CHOOSING ME

A PATH TO UNCONDITIONAL SELF-LOVE

CHOOSING ME

A PATH TO UNCONDITIONAL SELF-LOVE

JASK LEO

Bigfoot Publications
Because, there's a writer in everyone.

Choosing Me : A Path To Unconditional Self-Love
Author : Jask Leo

First Published by
Bigfoot06 Publications (OPC) Pvt. Ltd.
B-10,12 Shree Shyam Palace,
Sector 4,5 Chowk, Old Railway Road,
Gurugram, Haryana (122001)
Website: www.bigfootpublications.in
Email: info@bigfootpublications.in

First Edition : August, 2023

ISBN Print Book - **978-81-19512-22-5**

Printed in India

Shree Ganeshay Namaha

AUTHOR'S NOTE

Dear Reader,

Firstly, I want to express my gratitude for choosing to embark on this journey of self-love with me. The decision to prioritize yourself and cultivate a deep sense of love and acceptance is powerful, and I am honoured to be a part of your exploration.

This book is born out of my own personal experiences and the experiences of countless individuals who have embarked on the path of self-love. I understand the struggles, doubts, and moments of vulnerability that often accompany this journey. However, I also believe in the transformative power of self-love and its incredible impact on our lives.

Through these pages, I aim to offer you guidance, inspiration, and practical tools that will empower you to embrace yourself fully. My intention is not to provide a one-size-fits-all solution but rather to present a collection of strategies, stories, and exercises that can be adapted to your unique journey.

I invite you to approach this book with an open mind and an open heart. Take what resonates with you, and feel free to leave behind anything that doesn't serve you. Remember, you are the ultimate expert on your own life, and your intuition will guide you to the lessons and insights you most need at this moment.

I encourage you to approach this journey of self-love with kindness and patience. Like any worthwhile endeavours, it takes time and effort to cultivate self-love. There may be moments of doubt or setbacks along the way, but know that these are all part of the process. Trust in your own resilience and keep moving forward, one step at a time.

Lastly, I want to remind you that self-love is not selfish. In fact, it is a necessary foundation for creating healthy relationships, pursuing your dreams, and living a fulfilling life. By embracing and nurturing yourself, you are better able to show up fully for the people and causes that matter most to you.

Thank you again for choosing to walk this path of self-love. I am here to support you, cheer you on, and celebrate your victories. Together, let's create a world where self-love is not only accepted but celebrated as an essential aspect of our well-being.

With love and gratitude,

JASK

INTRODUCTION

In a world that often teaches us to prioritize others before ourselves, it's easy to forget the most important person in our lives - ourselves. True happiness and fulfilment come from within, from embracing our true selves with love, compassion, and acceptance. This is the essence of self-love.

"CHOOSING ME: A PATH TO UNCONDITIONAL SELF-LOVE" is a book that will guide you on this transformative journey. Through its pages, you will discover the power of self-love to heal, uplift, and empower your life in ways you never thought possible.

Join us as we explore the many dimensions of self-love, from nurturing your physical, mental, and emotional well-being, to cultivating deep self-acceptance and embracing your unique qualities. Through inspiring stories, practical exercises, and heartfelt advice, you will learn to let go of self-criticism, silence your inner doubter, and truly love yourself unconditionally.

This book is for anyone who has ever felt unworthy, unlovable, or lost. It's for those seeking to break free from the cycle of self-neglect, comparison, and people-pleasing. Whether you're just beginning your self-love journey or looking to deepen your existing practice, "Embrace Yourself" will be your trusted companion, guiding you every step of the way.

Within its pages, you will find:

- Strategies to quiet your inner critic and cultivate self-compassion
- Techniques to heal past wounds and embrace forgiveness
- Exercises to discover and embrace your authentic self
- Tools to establish healthy boundaries and prioritize your needs
- Inspiration to celebrate your successes, big and small
- Practices to nurture your mind, body, and soul
- Guidance on building positive relationships and surrounding yourself with uplifting people
- Affirmations and mantras to anchor your self-love practice

Remember, self-love is not a destination but a lifelong journey. It requires practice, patience, and a commitment to valuing and honouring yourself. When you learn to love yourself unconditionally, you unlock the door to a fulfilled, joyous, and purposeful life.

Are you ready to embark on this transformative journey of self-love? Let's begin.

TABLE OF CONTENTS

CHAPTER 1

UNDERSTANDING THE POWER OF SELF LOVE

BEGINNING OF OUR JOURNEY TO EXPLORE THE POWER OF SELF-LOVE: A SHORT STORY OF A SMALL-TOWN VILLAGE GIRL NAMED AARIA

Once upon a time, in a small village surrounded by a lush forest, there lived a young girl named Aria. Aria had always struggled with constantly comparing herself to others and feeling inadequate. One day, as she sat by a tranquil stream, she saw a wise old woman approaching. The old woman had a radiant aura, one that exuded self-love and acceptance.

The old woman saw Aaria and noticed that she was feeling sad about something. She approached Aaria and asked her what was wrong. Aaria told her that she felt that no one loved her and that there was nothing interesting left in her life. The old woman smiled and said, "My dear child, forget about others, do you love yourself? Self-love begins with embracing your uniqueness. You are a beautiful soul with your own set of talents and abilities. Embrace them with open arms and let go of comparison."

With those words, the old woman vanished, leaving Aaria deep in thought. Determined to embark on a journey of self-discovery, Aaria set out to find her true passions. She tried painting, dancing, and even learned to play the guitar, but none of them brought her joy.

Discouraged, Aaria returned to the stream, feeling defeated. As she sat there, gazing at her reflection in the water, she suddenly noticed the beauty of her own smile. Intrigued, she began to experiment with different expressions, discovering that each one conveyed a unique emotion.

In that moment, Aaria realized that she had a talent for expressing herself through her facial expressions. She had the power to light up a room with her smile, to comfort others with a compassionate gaze. This realization filled her with a newfound sense of self-love.

From that day forward, Aaria embraced her gift wholeheartedly. She started performing in local plays and spreading joy to those who watched her. As she shared her genuine smile, she began to see the impact it had on others - how it brightened their day and brought a sense of warmth and love into their lives.

Aaria's journey taught her that self-love is not about conforming to societal standards or trying to be someone else. It's about embracing and celebrating your own unique qualities, talents, and quirks. By confidently sharing her gifts with the world, Aaria not only found self-love but also inspired others to embrace their own uniqueness.

In the end, Aaria's power to spread love through her smile became a symbol of self-love and acceptance in her village. She started a movement, encouraging everyone to embrace their authentic selves and celebrate their individuality. Aaria's journey showed them that true happiness and fulfillment come from within, from loving oneself unconditionally.

And so, Aaria's story reminds us that self-love is not a destination but a journey. It is a journey of self-discovery, acceptance, and celebration. When we embrace and love ourselves for who we truly are, we become a beacon of light, spreading love and inspiration to those around us.

WHAT IS SELF-LOVE:

Self-love is the act of valuing and caring for oneself. It involves accepting and appreciating who you are, recognizing your worth and deservingness of love and happiness. Self-love involves treating yourself with kindness, compassion, and respect, prioritizing self-care and setting boundaries, and making choices that honor your well-being and personal growth. It is the foundation for building healthy relationships, pursuing your dreams and passions, and living a fulfilling and authentic life. Self-love is not selfish or narcissistic, but rather a necessary practice for personal happiness and overall well-being.

Self-love begins with acknowledging and celebrating your uniqueness. Embrace your strengths, quirks, and imperfections. Remember, you are one of a kind.

Also, self-love involves self-compassion. Treat yourself kindly and understand that it's okay to make mistakes.

Lastly, remember to shift your focus from external appearance to inner qualities and express yourself authentically.

Embracing self-love is a journey, but I know you have the strength to overcome any challenges along the way.

WHY IS SELF-LOVE IMPORTANT & BENEFITS OF PRACTICING SELF-LOVE:

Self-love is crucial for maintaining good mental health, forming healthy relationships, prioritizing self-care, fostering personal growth, building resilience, and achieving overall well-being and happiness. By embracing self-love, we cultivate a positive and fulfilling relationship with ourselves, which has a positive impact on all aspects of our lives.

BENEFITS OF PRACTICING SELF-LOVE:

Self-love is important for many reasons. Here are some key reasons why self-love is important:

1. **Improved mental health:** Self-love plays a crucial role in maintaining good mental health. When we love and accept ourselves, we are better equipped to deal with stress, overcome challenges, and maintain a positive outlook on life. Self-love helps reduce negative self-talk and self-criticism, leading to increased self-esteem and self-confidence.

2. **Healthy relationships:** When we practice self-love, we set healthy boundaries and become better at communicating our needs and desires. This allows us to form mutually respectful and fulfilling relationships with others. Self-love helps us attract healthy and positive relationships while deterring toxic or unhealthy ones.

3. **Increased self-care:** Self-love encourages us to prioritize our well-being. It reminds us to take care of our physical, emotional, and spiritual needs. By practicing self-care, we ensure that we are nourishing ourselves and cultivating a healthy and balanced lifestyle.

4. **Personal growth and self-improvement:** Self-love creates a foundation for personal growth and self-improvement. When we love ourselves, we are more motivated to pursue our dreams and goals, take risks, and step out of our comfort zones. Self-love promotes self-acceptance and empowers us to embrace our strengths and weaknesses, allowing for personal growth and development.

5. **Resilience and self-empowerment:** Self-love equips us with the resilience and self-empowerment needed to overcome

obstacles and bounce back from failures or setbacks. It strengthens our belief in our abilities and encourages us to persevere in the face of challenges.

6. **Overall well-being and happiness:** Ultimately, self-love leads to increased overall well-being and happiness. When we love ourselves, we have a higher sense of self-worth, contentment, and inner peace. We become our own greatest source of happiness and fulfilment, rather than relying on external validation.

Exercise : 1

Write about your understanding for self-love:

Write why self-love important for you:

Write your willingness (commitment statement) to practice self-love in your daily life:

CHAPTER 2
CULTIVATING SELF-ACCEPTANCE

Embracing Your Strengths and Weaknesses & Letting Go of Self-Judgment and Comparison

Embracing your strengths and weaknesses is an essential aspect of personal growth and self-acceptance. It allows you to develop a deeper understanding of yourself and build a strong foundation for success. Rather than viewing your weaknesses as flaws, you can see them as areas for improvement and opportunities for growth.

Firstly, it's important to recognize and appreciate your strengths. These are the qualities, skills, or talents that come naturally to you and set you apart from others. By acknowledging and embracing your strengths, you can build confidence, use them to your advantage, and excel in various areas of your life. Whether it's being a great communicator, being empathetic, or having a talent for problem-solving, your strengths are unique to you and can be harnessed to achieve your goals.

On the other hand, it's equally important to acknowledge and accept your weaknesses. Everyone has weaknesses, and it's unrealistic to expect perfection in every aspect of your life. Instead of feeling ashamed or discouraged by your weaknesses, view them as opportunities for personal growth. By recognizing your weaknesses, you can focus on areas that need improvement and actively work towards self-improvement. This might involve seeking additional training or education, asking for help from others, or practicing self-discipline and perseverance to overcome obstacles.

Embracing your strengths and weaknesses also involves understanding that they coexist and complement each other. Your weaknesses don't diminish your strengths, and your strengths can help mitigate your weaknesses. For example, if you're a great team player but struggle with public speaking, you can leverage your teamwork skills to collaborate with others and overcome your fear of public speaking. By embracing both your strengths and weaknesses, you develop a sense of self-awareness and authenticity that allows you to navigate life with confidence and resilience.

Furthermore, embracing your strengths and weaknesses can also foster a sense of empathy and understanding towards others. Recognizing that everyone has their own unique set of strengths and weaknesses encourages a non-judgmental and inclusive mindset. It allows you to appreciate the diversity of skills and abilities in others and creates a supportive and collaborative environment where everyone can thrive.

In conclusion, embracing your strengths and weaknesses is a powerful mindset that promotes personal growth, self-acceptance, and success. By acknowledging and appreciating your strengths, leveraging them to your advantage, and actively working on improving your weaknesses, you create a solid foundation for your personal and professional endeavors. Embracing your strengths and weaknesses also fosters empathy and understanding towards others, creating a supportive environment that encourages growth and collaboration. So, embrace your strengths, embrace your weaknesses, and embrace the journey of self-discovery and self-improvement.

Here comes a short story to shed more light on Embracing Your Strengths and Weaknesses and letting go of self-judgment and comparison. I kept it in a dramatical way:

EMMA, a young woman in her mid-20s, stands in front of a mirror, looking at herself with uncertainty. She appears unhappy and critical of her own reflection. EMMA picks up a notebook and a pen, determined to change her perspective.

EMMA opens a motivational chat with her SELF-LOVE COACH, JASON. Jason's name appears on the screen.

JASON (via text): Hello, Emma! How can I support you today?

EMMA (typing): Hey, Jason. I'm struggling with accepting and loving myself unconditionally. I always find flaws and beat myself up over them. I need help embracing unconditional self-love.

JASON (via text): I understand, Emma. Remember, unconditional self-love is a journey. Let's explore some strategies together.

EMMA looks hopeful and eagerly waits for JASON's guidance.

JASON (V.O.): Emma, it starts with practicing self-compassion and understanding your strengths and weaknesses. Treat yourself as you would a dear friend going through a difficult time.

EMMA (nodding): I can definitely try being more compassionate toward myself. It's time to be my own best friend and explore more about me, about my strengths, and weaknesses.

JASON (V.O.): That's the spirit, Emma! Now, let's focus on self-acceptance. Embrace all aspects of yourself, even the ones you consider flaws. They make you unique.

EMMA (taking a deep breath): I've spent so long fighting against my "flaws." It's time to accept them as a part of who I am.

JASON (V.O.): Wonderful! Moving forward, replace self-criticism with self-appreciation. Celebrate your accomplishments, no matter how big or small.

EMMA smiles, feeling a sense of relief.

EMMA (gratefully): I've never really acknowledged my own achievements before. It's time to give myself credit for the progress I've made.

JASON (V.O.): Yes, Emma! Remember, you deserve love and kindness in all aspects of your life, including your relationships. Surround yourself with those who support and uplift you.

EMMA (feeling empowered): You're right, Jason. I need to let go of toxic relationships and seek connections that nourish my soul.

JASON (V.O.): Absolutely, Emma! Lastly, set healthy boundaries to protect your emotional well-being. Prioritize your needs and say "no" when necessary.

EMMA takes a moment to reflect, ready to make positive changes.

EMMA (determined): I've neglected my own boundaries for far too long. It's time to prioritize my well-being and start saying "no" when it's necessary.

JASON (V.O.): That's amazing, Emma! Embracing unconditional self-love is a journey, but I believe in you.

EMMA looks at herself in the mirror, feeling a newfound sense of self-acceptance and love.

EMMA (confidently): Thank you, Jason! I'm ready to embark on this journey of unconditional self-love. I deserve it.

FADE OUT.

Umm! Interesting conversation between EMMA and JASON, right? I am sure this will definitely inspire you to take the first step towards your Self-love journey.

Finding Beauty in Imperfection

In a world that constantly emphasizes perfection and flawlessness, finding beauty in imperfection is a profound and liberating concept. It is about recognizing and embracing the uniqueness and authenticity that lie within every person, object, or situation – imperfections and all.

To find beauty in imperfection, we must shift our perspective and challenge society's narrow definition of beauty. Instead of striving for an unattainable standard of flawlessness, we can celebrate the beauty that arises from the quirks, flaws, and idiosyncrasies that make us who we are.

One way to find beauty in imperfection is through the art of wabi-sabi, a Japanese aesthetic philosophy that values the beauty of impermanence, imperfection, and the incomplete. It encourages us to appreciate the natural processes of aging, weathering, and decay, seeing them as inherent parts of life's journey. By embracing the imperfections and finding beauty in them, we can discover a deeper sense of connection with the world around us.

In nature, we can find abundant examples of the beauty of imperfection. Whether it's a gnarled tree in a forest, a wildflower growing amidst a bed of weeds, or the asymmetrical patterns on a seashell, nature showcases the beauty that exists beyond conventional standards of perfection. The imperfections found in natural objects remind us of the constant ebb and flow of life and the resilience that comes from adapting to change.

On a personal level, finding beauty in imperfection means valuing the journey of self-growth and embracing our own flaws and mistakes as opportunities for learning and growth. It means accepting that we are not always going to be perfect and that it is okay to make mistakes. In fact, our imperfections can often teach us important lessons about resilience, empathy, and self-compassion.

In relationships, finding beauty in imperfection means accepting and celebrating the humanity of others. It means recognizing that everyone has their own idiosyncrasies, insecurities, and imperfections, and seeing them as part of what makes them uniquely beautiful. By embracing the imperfections of others, we can foster deeper connections and create more compassionate and accepting relationships.

Ultimately, finding beauty in imperfection is about shifting our mindset and embracing a more holistic and inclusive definition of beauty. It is about cherishing the inherent beauty that lies within all things, beyond superficial appearances. It is about recognizing the depth, resilience, and authenticity that comes from embracing imperfection. And in doing so, we can cultivate a more compassionate, accepting, and joyful outlook on life.

Exercise : 2

Write your Strengths and Weakness:

Strengths:

1. ____________________

   ____

2. ____________________

   ____

3. ____________________

   ____

4. ____________________

   ____

5. ____________________

   ____

Weakness:

1. ____________________

   ____

2. ____________________

   ____

3. ____________________

   ____

4. ____________________

   ____

5. ____________________

   ____

How would you turn your Flaws (weakness) in positive way:

Make a bold statement about self (How you feel about yourself) – your current mindset.

CHAPTER 3

PRIORITIZING SELF-CARE AND SELF-COMPASSION

Nurturing Your Well-being: Prioritizing Self-Care and Self-Compassion

In today's fast-paced and demanding world, it's easy to get caught up in the busyness of life and neglect our own well-being. However, practicing self-care and self-compassion is essential for maintaining our physical, mental, and emotional health. By prioritizing ourselves and dedicating time to self-care, we can cultivate a sense of balance, replenish our energy, and foster a positive relationship with ourselves. In this chapter, we will explore the importance of self-care and self-compassion and provide practical strategies for incorporating them into your daily life.

Understanding Self-Care: Self-care encompasses a range of activities and practices that promote overall well-being. It involves taking intentional actions to nurture and restore ourselves physically, mentally, and emotionally. Self-care is not a luxury or selfish indulgence but a vital necessity for leading a fulfilling life. Recognizing the importance of self-care is the first step towards prioritizing it in your routine.

The Power of Self-Compassion: Self-compassion involves treating ourselves with kindness, understanding, and acceptance, especially during challenging times. It entails acknowledging our imperfections, embracing our humanity, and offering ourselves the same compassion we would extend to others. Practicing self-compassion cultivates resilience, reduces self-judgment, and enhances our overall well-being.

Prioritizing Self-Care and Self-Compassion:

a. **Assess your needs:** Take time to reflect on your physical, mental, and emotional needs. Identify activities and practices that bring you joy, relaxation, and fulfillment. Make a list of self-care activities that resonate with you.

b. **Set boundaries:** Learn to say no to activities or commitments that drain your energy or overwhelm you. Establish healthy boundaries to protect your time, energy, and well-being.

c. **Schedule self-care:** Make self-care a non-negotiable part of your routine. Block out dedicated time on your calendar for self-care activities and treat them as important appointments with yourself.

d. **Start small:** Incorporate small, manageable self-care practices into your daily life. It can be as simple as taking short breaks to stretch, enjoying a cup of tea, or spending a few minutes in meditation or deep breathing.

e. **Practice self-compassion:** Be kind and gentle with yourself, especially during difficult moments. Replace self-criticism with self-compassionate thoughts and affirmations. Treat yourself with the same care and understanding you would offer to a dear friend.

f. **Engage in activities you love:** Make time for hobbies, creative pursuits, and activities that bring you joy. Engaging in activities you love enhances your sense of self-worth and fulfillment.

g. Seek support: Reach out to loved ones or seek professional help when needed. Surround yourself with a supportive network that encourages your self-care journey.

Overcoming Barriers:

a. Guilt and self-judgment: Recognize that self-care is not selfish but necessary for your well-being. Release guilt and let go of self-judgment. Remember that by taking care of yourself, you become better equipped to care for others.

b. Time constraints: Start by carving out small pockets of time for self-care. Look for opportunities throughout your day, such as during your commute or lunch break, to incorporate self-care practices. Prioritize and make self-care a priority, even if it means delegating or outsourcing certain tasks.

c. Mindset shift: Challenge societal narratives that equate productivity with self-worth. Embrace the belief that self-care and self-compassion are essential investments in your long-term health and happiness.

Prioritizing self-care and self-compassion is not a luxury; it is a fundamental aspect of leading a healthy and fulfilling life. By making self-care a priority and nurturing self-compassion, you can replenish your energy, enhance your well-being, and cultivate a positive relationship with yourself. Remember, you deserve care, compassion, and love – from others and, most importantly, from yourself. Start small, be consistent, and watch how prioritizing your well-being transforms your life for the better.

Practices for Mental and Emotional Well-being:

Cultivating Mental and Emotional Well-being - Essential Practices

Introduction: In today's fast-paced and often stressful world, prioritizing mental and emotional well-being is crucial for maintaining a balanced and fulfilling life. By incorporating specific practices into our daily routine, we can nurture our mental and emotional health, build resilience, and experience greater overall well-being. In this chapter, we will explore some practical practices that can support and enhance your mental and emotional well-being.

1. **Mindfulness and Meditation:** Engaging in mindfulness and meditation practices can help calm the mind, reduce stress, and increase self-awareness. Set aside a few minutes each day to focus on your breath, observe your thoughts without judgment, and cultivate a sense of presence. Whether through guided meditation, breathwork exercises, or mindful activities like walking or eating, these practices can promote a sense of inner peace and clarity.

2. **Journaling:** Writing down your thoughts and emotions in a journal can be a powerful tool for self-reflection and emotional release. Dedicate regular time to journaling, allowing yourself to freely express your thoughts, feelings, and experiences. This practice can help gain insights, process emotions, and foster self-discovery.

3. **Engaging in Physical Activity:** Regular physical exercise is not only beneficial for physical health but also plays a vital role in promoting mental and emotional well-being. Engage in activities you enjoy, whether it's walking, jogging, dancing, or practicing yoga. Physical exercise releases endorphins, reduces stress hormones, and enhances mood, leading to improved mental and emotional states.

i. **Nurturing Healthy Relationships:** Nurturing healthy relationships is essential for mental and emotional well-being. Surround yourself with supportive and positive individuals who uplift and inspire you. Seek opportunities to connect with loved ones, friends, or support groups. Engage in open and honest communication, practice active listening, and offer support to others. Meaningful connections contribute to a sense of belonging and provide a valuable support system during challenging times.

ii. **Establishing Healthy Boundaries:** Establishing healthy boundaries is crucial for protecting your mental and emotional well-being. Learn to say no when necessary and communicate your needs and limits to others. Respect your personal space and time, and prioritize self-care activities that nourish your mind and emotions. Setting boundaries promotes self-respect, reduces stress, and helps maintain a healthy balance in relationships.

iii. **Practicing Self-Compassion:** Treat yourself with kindness, understanding, and self-compassion. Acknowledge your strengths and imperfections without self-judgment. When faced with challenges or setbacks, offer yourself the same empathy and support you would extend to a friend. Embrace self-care practices, positive affirmations, and self-encouragement. Cultivating self-compassion enhances resilience, reduces stress, and fosters a positive self-image.

iv. **Managing Media Consumption:** In today's digital age, excessive exposure to media can contribute to stress, anxiety, and feelings of inadequacy. Take breaks from social media, news, and other forms of media that may be overwhelming or triggering. Create a healthy balance by setting boundaries around your media consumption and engaging in activities that nourish your mind and emotions offline.

v. **Seeking Professional Support:** If you are experiencing persistent or severe mental or emotional challenges, seeking professional support is essential. Consult with a therapist, counsellor, or mental health professional who can provide guidance, support, and evidence-based interventions to address your specific needs.

Prioritizing mental and emotional well-being is a transformative practice that allows us to navigate life's challenges with resilience and balance. By incorporating these practices into our daily lives, such as mindfulness, journaling, physical activity, healthy relationships, setting boundaries, self-compassion, managing media consumption, and seeking professional support when needed, we can nurture our mental and emotional health and experience a greater sense of well-being and fulfilment. Remember, your mental and emotional well-being matters, and investing in it is a lifelong journey worth pursuing.

Taking Care of Your Physical Health and Wellness

The Path to Optimal Physical Health and Wellness: Taking Care of Your Body

Caring for your physical health and wellness is a fundamental aspect of leading a vibrant and fulfilling life. By prioritizing your body's well-being through healthy habits and self-care practices, you can enhance your energy levels, improve overall functioning, and foster a greater sense of vitality. In this chapter, we will explore practical strategies for taking care of your physical health and wellness, empowering you to embrace a lifestyle that supports your body's needs.

1. **Balanced Nutrition:** Fueling your body with a balanced and nutritious diet is essential for optimal physical health. Focus on consuming whole foods, including a variety of fruits, vegetables, whole grains, lean proteins, and healthy fats. Limit processed foods, sugar, and excessive salt intake. Stay hydrated by drinking an adequate amount of water throughout the day. Aim for portion control and mindful eating, paying attention to hunger and fullness cues.

2. **Regular Physical Activity:** Engaging in regular physical activity is key to maintaining a healthy body and mind. Find activities that you enjoy and that suit your fitness level and preferences, whether it's brisk walking, jogging, dancing, cycling, swimming, or practicing yoga. Aim for at least 150 minutes of moderate-intensity aerobic exercise or 75 minutes

of vigorous-intensity exercise per week. Incorporate strength training exercises to improve muscle strength and endurance. Remember to consult with a healthcare professional before starting any new exercise program.

3. **Sufficient Rest and Sleep:** Prioritizing quality rest and sleep is crucial for your physical health and overall well-being. Aim for 7-9 hours of sleep each night, ensuring a comfortable sleep environment and establishing a consistent bedtime routine. Create a relaxing atmosphere by practicing relaxation techniques, such as deep breathing, meditation, or gentle stretching before bed. Adequate rest and sleep promote proper immune function, enhance cognitive performance, and support overall physical recovery.

4. **Stress Management:** Chronic stress can take a toll on your physical health. Implement stress management techniques to reduce its impact on your body. Engage in activities that help you unwind and relax, such as taking regular breaks, practicing mindfulness, spending time in nature, or pursuing hobbies and interests. Cultivate a support system and seek social connections to share your experiences and seek guidance when needed.

5. **Regular Health Check-ups:** Schedule regular check-ups with your healthcare provider to monitor your overall health and address any potential concerns. Stay up-to-date with immunizations, screenings, and preventive measures. Discuss any lifestyle changes or concerns with your healthcare professional, who can provide personalized guidance and support.

6. **Hygiene and Self-Care:** Maintaining proper hygiene practices is essential for physical health and well-being. Practice good hand hygiene, maintain oral health through regular brushing and flossing, and adhere to personal care routines. Prioritize self-care activities that make you feel good, such as taking relaxing baths, pampering your skin, or

engaging in activities that promote relaxation and stress relief.

7. **Limiting Substance Use:** Limit or avoid the use of substances that can negatively impact your physical health, such as tobacco, excessive alcohol, and illicit drugs. If you need support in managing substance use, reach out to healthcare professionals or support groups that can provide assistance.

8. **Listening to Your Body:** Pay attention to the signals your body sends. Rest when you're fatigued, address any pain or discomfort promptly, and give yourself time to recover from illness or injury. Be mindful of your body's needs, such as proper hydration and nutrition, and make adjustments to your habits and routines accordingly.

Taking care of your physical health and wellness is a lifelong commitment that empowers you to live life to the fullest. By embracing a balanced diet, engaging in regular physical activity, prioritizing rest and sleep, managing stress, attending regular health check-ups, practicing good hygiene, limiting substance use, and listening to your body's cues, you can optimize your physical well-being. Remember, your body is your greatest asset, and investing in its care and maintenance allows you to thrive and enjoy a healthier, more vibrant life.

Self love

15 WAYS TO PRACTICE

MIND

1. Write yourself a love letter
2. Make a list of 10 things you're grateful for
3. Buy yourself a bouquet of flowers
4. Re-read your favorite book
5. Create a vision board for your dreams

BODY

6. Have a pamper sesh and treat yourself to a mani/pedi
7. Take a 30 minute walk in nature
8. Take a long relaxing bubble bath
9. Try relaxing yoga or an empowering workout
10. Nourish your body with a healthy home cooked meal

SOUL

11. Create loving, positive affirmations for yourself
12. Slow down, be present and mindful
13. Make a list of 10 things you love about yourself
14. Unplug for a whole day from any tech
15. Meditate

Exercise : 3

Write what action you will be taking for Physical and Mental wellness:

CHAPTER 4

HEALING PAST WOUNDS AND FORGIVING YOURSELF

Liberating Yourself: Identifying and Releasing Emotional Baggage

Emotional baggage refers to unresolved emotions, past traumas, negative beliefs, and recurring patterns that we carry within ourselves. These unresolved emotions can hinder our personal growth, relationships, and overall well-being. Identifying and releasing emotional baggage is an empowering process that allows us to heal, cultivate emotional freedom, and create space for positive experiences. In this article, we will explore effective strategies for identifying and releasing emotional baggage, enabling you to embark on a journey of healing and personal transformation.

1. **Self-Reflection and Awareness:** Begin by developing self-awareness and the willingness to explore your emotions and past experiences. Reflect on your thoughts, feelings, and behaviors, and identify any recurring patterns or unresolved emotions that may be causing emotional baggage. Journaling, therapy, meditation, and self-reflection exercises can help deepen your understanding of your emotions and uncover hidden wounds.

2. **Identify Emotional Triggers:** Pay attention to situations, people, or events that trigger intense emotional reactions within you. These triggers often indicate unresolved emotional baggage related to past experiences. Notice when you feel anger, sadness, fear, or other strong emotions, and explore the underlying causes and connections to your past. By identifying your triggers, you can begin to unravel the emotional baggage attached to them.

3. **Practice Emotional Release:** Emotional release is a vital step in letting go of emotional baggage. Find healthy ways to express your emotions, such as through journaling, talking to a trusted friend or therapist, engaging in creative outlets like art or music, or practicing physical activities that allow you to release pent-up emotions, such as running or dancing. Allow yourself to fully experience and express your emotions without judgment or suppression.

4. **Forgiveness:** Forgiveness is a transformative practice that liberates us from emotional baggage. Forgive yourself for any mistakes or shortcomings, and extend forgiveness to others who may have hurt you. Remember that forgiveness does not mean condoning hurtful actions; it is about freeing yourself from the emotional burden associated with those actions. Practice self-compassion and empathy towards yourself and others, fostering healing and emotional release.

5. **Letting Go of Negative Beliefs:** Examine any negative beliefs you hold about yourself, others, or the world. These beliefs often stem from past experiences and can perpetuate emotional baggage. Challenge and reframe negative beliefs by seeking evidence to the contrary, replacing them with positive affirmations, and cultivating self-compassion and self-love. Embrace empowering beliefs that support your emotional well-being and growth.

6. **Seek Support:** Healing emotional baggage can be a challenging journey, and seeking support is essential. Reach out to trusted friends, family members, or a therapist who can

provide guidance, validation, and a safe space to explore and process your emotions. Professional support can be particularly beneficial when dealing with deep-rooted emotional wounds.

7. **Practice Self-Care:** Prioritize self-care practices that nourish your mind, body, and soul. Engage in activities that promote relaxation, stress reduction, and self-compassion, such as practicing mindfulness, engaging in hobbies you enjoy, spending time in nature, or engaging in regular exercise. Self-care provides a foundation of well-being and resilience as you navigate the process of releasing emotional baggage.

Identifying and releasing emotional baggage is a transformative journey towards emotional freedom and personal growth. By developing self-awareness, identifying emotional triggers, practicing emotional release, forgiveness, letting go of negative beliefs, seeking support, and prioritizing self-care, you can release the weight of past experiences and create space for healing and positive transformations. Embrace this journey with patience, self-compassion, and an open heart, and watch as you step into a brighter and more liberated future. Remember, you have the power to release emotional baggage and cultivate a life filled with emotional well-being and joy.

Embracing Forgiveness and Letting Go of Resentment

Forgiveness and releasing resentment are powerful acts of liberation that can transform our emotional well-being and free us from the burdens of the past. Holding onto resentment can weigh heavily on our hearts and minds, hindering personal growth and hindering our ability to experience true happiness and inner peace. In this article, we will explore the importance of embracing forgiveness, offer insights into the process of letting go of resentment, and provide practical strategies for cultivating forgiveness in your life.

1. **Understanding Forgiveness:** Forgiveness is not about condoning or forgetting the hurtful actions of others; it is a conscious choice to release the emotional burden and negative energy associated with past experiences. It is an act of compassion and self-liberation that empowers us to break free from the cycle of resentment and find healing.

2. **Acknowledge and Validate Your Feelings:** Before forgiveness can take place, it is essential to acknowledge and validate your feelings of anger, hurt, or betrayal. Allow yourself to feel and express these emotions in a healthy way, whether through journaling, talking to a trusted friend, or seeking professional support. Recognize that your feelings are valid and deserve acknowledgment.

3. **Cultivate Empathy and Compassion:** Developing empathy and compassion towards yourself and others involved in the situation is a vital step in the forgiveness process. Try to understand the perspectives, motivations, and struggles of those who have hurt you. Recognize that people are fallible, capable of making mistakes, and often acting from their own pain or limitations. Cultivating empathy and compassion helps shift your perspective and softens the barriers to forgiveness.

4. **Release the Need for Control:** Resentment often stems from a desire to control the outcome or seek justice for the past. However, holding onto this need for control only perpetuates negative emotions and prevents forgiveness. Let go of the desire to change the past or seek revenge, realizing that you cannot control the actions or choices of others. Focus instead on your own growth and well-being.

5. **Practice Self-Reflection:** Engage in self-reflection to gain deeper insights into your own role in the situation and your emotional reactions. Explore any patterns, triggers, or unresolved wounds that may be contributing to your resentment. Taking responsibility for your own emotions and

reactions allows you to reclaim your power and make choices that lead to healing and forgiveness.

6. **Choose Forgiveness:** Forgiveness is a conscious choice that you can make for yourself. Decide to let go of the resentment and commit to the process of forgiveness. Understand that forgiveness is a journey and it may take time. Be patient and gentle with yourself as you navigate through the emotions and challenges that may arise along the way.

7. **Practice Self-Forgiveness:** Alongside forgiving others, it is crucial to extend forgiveness to yourself. Recognize that you are human and capable of making mistakes. Release self-blame and self-judgment, and offer yourself the same compassion and understanding you would extend to others. Embrace self-forgiveness as an integral part of your healing journey.

8. **Release and Heal:** Release the emotional baggage by actively working on letting go of resentment. Practice forgiveness rituals such as writing a forgiveness letter (even if you don't send it), visualization exercises, or engaging in therapeutic techniques like meditation or forgiveness affirmations. Engage in activities that promote healing, self-care, and self-discovery to support your journey toward forgiveness.

Embracing forgiveness and letting go of resentment is a transformative process that allows us to reclaim our emotional freedom and create space for healing and personal growth. By acknowledging our feelings, cultivating empathy and compassion, releasing the need for control, practicing self-reflection, choosing forgiveness, practicing self-forgiveness, and actively releasing resentment, we can experience the liberation that forgiveness brings. Remember that forgiveness is a gift you give yourself, freeing you from the weight of the past and opening up the possibility for a brighter and more peaceful future.

Moving Forward with Compassion and Grace: Embracing Growth and Resilience

Moving forward in life requires a balance of compassion and grace, both towards ourselves and others. It involves embracing the lessons learned from the past, cultivating self-compassion, and extending understanding and empathy to those around us. By adopting a mindset of compassion and grace, we can navigate challenges, foster personal growth, and build strong, meaningful relationships. In this article, we will explore the importance of moving forward with compassion and grace and provide practical strategies for embracing these qualities in our daily lives.

1. **Embrace Self-Compassion:** Start by cultivating self-compassion as the foundation for moving forward with grace. Treat yourself with kindness, understanding, and forgiveness. Acknowledge that everyone makes mistakes and experiences setbacks. Practice self-care, engage in positive self-talk, and let go of self-judgment. Embracing self-compassion allows you to learn from your experiences without dwelling on self-criticism and negativity.

2. **Learn from Past Experiences:** Reflect on past experiences and challenges as opportunities for growth and learning. Rather than dwelling on regrets or resentments, focus on the lessons and insights gained from those experiences. Use these lessons to make informed choices and navigate future situations with greater wisdom and resilience.

3. **Cultivate Empathy and Understanding:** Extend compassion and empathy to others by seeking to understand their perspectives and experiences. Recognize that everyone is on their own unique journey, facing their own struggles and challenges. Practice active listening, suspend judgment, and strive to see situations from different points of view. Cultivating empathy fosters deeper connections, promotes understanding, and encourages compassion-driven actions.

4. **Practice Forgiveness:** Forgiveness is a powerful act of grace that liberates both parties involved. Release resentment and grudges by choosing forgiveness, not for the sake of others, but for your own emotional well-being. Understand that forgiveness does not mean condoning harmful actions, but rather freeing yourself from the burden of anger and bitterness. Practice forgiveness towards others and yourself to foster inner peace and growth.

5. **Let Go of Control:**

a) **Accept that there are aspects of life beyond your control.** Embrace uncertainty with grace, understanding that change is a natural part of life. Focus on what you can control, such as your attitude, actions, and responses. Surrender the need for perfection and allow space for flexibility and adaptation. Letting go of the need for control enables you to move forward with resilience and openness.

b) **Set Healthy Boundaries:** Establishing healthy boundaries is an act of self-care and respect. Clearly define your limits and communicate them to others in a compassionate manner. Setting boundaries allows you to protect your well-being, honor your values, and maintain healthy relationships. Embrace the courage to say no when necessary and prioritize your own needs and desires.

c) **Practice Gratitude:** Cultivate a sense of gratitude for the present moment and the blessings in your life. Focus on what you have rather than what you lack. Regularly express gratitude to yourself and others for their contributions, support, and presence. Practicing gratitude fosters a positive mindset, resilience, and appreciation for the journey ahead.

d) **Embrace Growth Mindset:** Adopt a growth mindset, recognizing that personal growth is a lifelong journey. Embrace challenges as opportunities for learning and development. Embrace a positive attitude towards change and view setbacks as stepping stones towards success. Embracing a growth mindset allows you to approach life with curiosity, resilience, and an eagerness to learn and evolve.

Moving forward with compassion and grace empowers us to navigate life's challenges with resilience, understanding, and empathy. By cultivating self-compassion, learning from the past, extending empathy, practicing forgiveness, letting go of control, setting healthy boundaries, practicing gratitude, and embracing a growth mindset, we can embrace personal growth and build meaningful connections with others. Remember, moving forward with compassion and grace is a transformative practice that leads to greater fulfillment, inner peace, and the ability to embrace life's journey with open arms.

Exercise : 4

Every day read the below affirmations for releasing emotional baggage:

1. I release the past and embrace forgiveness with an open heart and mind.
2. I forgive myself for any mistakes I've made and choose to grow from them.
3. I release any resentment or anger towards others, and I free myself from their hold on my emotions.
4. I am worthy of healing, and I choose to forgive those who have caused me pain.
5. I let go of old grudges and open myself to the peace that forgiveness brings.
6. I release the past and step into the present with a renewed sense of freedom.
7. Forgiving others sets me free from the weight of negativity and empowers my spirit.
8. Each day, I am releasing the past and embracing a brighter future.
9. Forgiveness is a gift I give to myself, allowing me to move forward with grace and compassion.
10. I am capable of forgiving, and forgiveness is a strength that sets me free.
11. My heart is open to forgiveness, and I choose to release any barriers that block its flow.
12. I release any pain from the past and choose to create a loving and peaceful future.

13. I forgive others not because they deserve it, but because I deserve peace and happiness.
14. I am not defined by my past; I am empowered by my ability to forgive and let go.
15. Forgiveness is a process, and I am patient with myself as I release past wounds.
16. I release any self-judgment and forgive myself for any perceived shortcomings.
17. I am resilient and capable of releasing old barriers to embrace new opportunities.
18. Forgiveness is my key to freedom, and I unlock it with love and understanding.
19. As I forgive others, I am also forgiving myself and allowing healing to flow through me.
20. I am choosing love over resentment, and forgiveness over bitterness.

One more action needed: Before you read these affirmations, take a pen and paper, write down all your past bad memories, bad experiences, worries, and sorrows. Once you finish writing, take out all the feelings which you kept inside you for so long, look at the paper once again, and tear it into small pieces and throw it in the dustbin or fire it and burn it all the way. You will feel relaxed and light on your heart. It's a very impactful action that will give you mental relaxation.

CHAPTER 5

SETTING BOUNDARIES AND PRIORITIZING YOUR NEEDS

Building Healthy Relationships: Establishing Boundaries with Respect and Care

Establishing healthy boundaries is vital for fostering positive and fulfilling relationships. Boundaries serve as guidelines that define and protect our emotional, physical, and mental well-being, enabling us to maintain a sense of self-respect, autonomy, and healthy connection with others. In this article, we will explore the importance of establishing healthy boundaries in relationships and provide practical strategies for communicating and maintaining them.

1. **Understand Your Needs:** Begin by reflecting on your own needs, values, and limits. Take time to identify what makes you feel comfortable, respected, and emotionally safe within relationships. Consider your emotional, physical, and mental boundaries, and understand that they may evolve over time. Self-awareness is key to effectively communicating your boundaries to others.

2. **Communicate Openly and Clearly:** Clearly express your boundaries to others in a calm and assertive manner. Use "I"

statements to express how specific behaviours or actions affect you. Be direct and specific about what is acceptable and what is not. Avoid blaming or criticizing others and focus on expressing your needs and expectations. Effective communication helps others understand and respect your boundaries.

3. **Trust Your Intuition:** Listen to your instincts and trust your feelings when something doesn't feel right. If a situation or relationship consistently leaves you feeling uncomfortable, disrespected, or compromised, it may be an indication that your boundaries are being crossed. Trusting your intuition empowers you to honour your own well-being and make decisions that align with your values.

4. **Practice Self-Care:** Nurture your own self-care as a way to maintain healthy boundaries in relationships. Prioritize activities that replenish and energize you. Set aside time for self-reflection, engage in hobbies, practice self-compassion, and establish routines that support your physical and emotional well-being. Taking care of yourself strengthens your ability to establish and maintain boundaries with others.

5. **Learn to Say No:** Saying no is an essential part of setting boundaries. Understand that it is okay to decline requests or activities that do not align with your needs, values, or time constraints. Assertively and kindly communicate your limits, without feeling guilty or obligated to please others. Remember, saying no is an act of self-care and respect for yourself and your boundaries.

6. **Establish Consequences:** It's crucial to establish consequences for when your boundaries are disregarded or crossed. Clearly communicate the consequences to others in advance, ensuring they understand the potential outcomes if boundaries are violated. Consistently follow through with the consequences you've established to maintain the integrity of your boundaries and reinforce healthy relationship dynamics.

7. **Seek Support:** Seek support from trusted friends, family members, or professionals when navigating challenging relationship dynamics. Discuss your experiences and concerns with someone who can provide guidance and understanding. Supportive individuals can offer different perspectives and help validate your boundaries, reinforcing your confidence in maintaining them.

8. **Regularly Revisit and Adjust Boundaries:** Boundaries are not static; they may evolve as you grow and change. Regularly assess and reassess your boundaries to ensure they align with your current needs and values. Communicate any adjustments or changes in boundaries with the relevant individuals, fostering open and ongoing dialogue within your relationships.

Establishing healthy boundaries in relationships is crucial for fostering respect, trust, and overall well-being. By understanding your needs, communicating openly, trusting your intuition, practicing self-care, learning to say no, establishing consequences, seeking support, and regularly reviewing and adjusting boundaries, you can cultivate relationships that honour your individuality and promote mutual respect. Remember, setting and maintaining healthy boundaries is an ongoing process that empowers you to build authentic and fulfilling connections with others while honouring your own well-being.

Embracing the Power of "No": Saying It with Confidence and Self-Respect

Saying "no" is an essential skill that allows us to set boundaries, protect our well-being, and prioritize our own needs and values. However, many people struggle with asserting this simple word confidently and without guilt. By learning to say "no" with confidence and self-respect, we empower ourselves to lead a more balanced and fulfilling life. In this article, we will explore the importance of saying "no," provide practical strategies for asserting it with confidence, and discuss the positive impact it can have on our overall well-being.

1. **Recognize the Importance of Saying "No":** Understand that saying "no" is a powerful act of self-care and self-respect. It allows you to honor your own boundaries, protect your time and energy, and maintain a healthy balance in your life. Realize that by saying "no" to certain things, you create space for "yes" to the activities, commitments, and relationships that truly align with your values and priorities.

2. **Cultivate Self-Awareness:** Develop a clear understanding of your own needs, values, and limits. Reflect on what is truly important to you and the impact certain requests or commitments may have on your overall well-being. Knowing yourself and your boundaries will give you the confidence to say "no" when something doesn't align with your values or compromises your personal boundaries.

3. **Practice Assertiveness:** Assertiveness is key to saying "no" with confidence. Be direct, clear, and respectful in your communication. Use "I" statements to express your thoughts and feelings. Avoid excessive apologies or long explanations. Keep your response concise and to the point, without feeling the need to justify or defend your decision.

4. **Set Boundaries and Prioritize:** Establish clear boundaries that reflect your needs and values. Prioritize your commitments and obligations, recognizing that you cannot do everything for everyone. Understand that saying "no" to certain requests allows you to focus on what truly matters to you and maintain a healthy balance in your life. Setting boundaries helps you establish guidelines for when and how to say "no" confidently.

5. **Practice Saying "No":** Just like any other skill, saying "no" becomes easier with practice. Start by saying "no" to smaller requests or commitments that are less important to you. As you gain confidence, gradually tackle more significant or

challenging situations. Remember that practice is about progress, not perfection. Celebrate your efforts and growth along the way.

6. **Use Positive Language:** Frame your "no" in a positive light to maintain respectful and constructive communication. Offer alternative solutions, if possible, or express appreciation for the opportunity. For example, "I'm unable to commit to this project right now, but I appreciate you considering me. Perhaps we can explore other options or collaborate in the future."

7. **Manage Guilt and Self-Doubt:** Guilt and self-doubt are common emotions that may arise when saying "no." Recognize that it is normal to feel this way, but remember that your well-being is a priority. Remind yourself that saying "no" is not a rejection of others but a way to honor your own needs. Practice self-compassion and remind yourself that you deserve to set boundaries and prioritize self-care.

8. **Surround Yourself with Supportive People:** Surround yourself with individuals who respect your boundaries and encourage you to prioritize your well-being. Seek support from friends, family, or mentors who understand the importance of saying "no" and can offer guidance and encouragement. Having a supportive network will reinforce your confidence in asserting your boundaries.

Saying "no" with confidence and self-respect is an essential skill that allows us to protect our well-being, honour our boundaries, and lead a more balanced and fulfilling life. By recognizing the importance of saying "no," cultivating self-awareness, practicing assertiveness, setting boundaries, using positive language, managing guilt and self-doubt, and surrounding yourself with supportive people, you can embrace the power of "no" and create a life that aligns with your values and priorities. Remember, saying "no" is an act of self-care and empowerment that ultimately leads to greater fulfilment and a healthier, more balanced existence.

Prioritizing Yourself without Guilt: Embracing Self-Care and Well-being

Putting yourself first is not selfish; it is an essential act of self-care that allows you to nurture your physical, mental, and emotional well-being. However, many people struggle with guilt when prioritizing themselves over others' needs and expectations. By learning to put yourself first without guilt, you can cultivate a healthier, more balanced life that supports your overall well-being. In this article, we will explore the importance of prioritizing yourself, provide practical strategies for overcoming guilt, and discuss the positive impact it can have on your overall happiness and fulfilment.

1. **Understand the Importance of Self-Care:** Recognize that self-care is not a luxury but a necessity. Putting yourself first allows you to recharge, replenish your energy, and maintain a strong foundation for your physical, mental, and emotional well-being. Understand that by taking care of yourself, you become better equipped to show up for others and meet their needs effectively.

2. **Acknowledge Your Needs and Values:** Gain clarity about your own needs, values, and priorities. Reflect on what truly matters to you and what brings you joy, fulfilment, and a sense of purpose. Understand that by honouring your needs, you are creating a life that aligns with your values and supports your overall well-being.

3. **Set Boundaries and Communicate Them:** Establish clear boundaries to protect your time, energy, and well-being. Communicate these boundaries assertively and respectfully to others. Clearly express your needs and limitations, and be firm in upholding them. Remember that setting boundaries is

not a selfish act, but a way to ensure that your well-being is prioritized.

4. **Practice Self-Compassion:** Release guilt by practicing self-compassion. Treat yourself with kindness, understanding, and acceptance. Remind yourself that it is okay to prioritize yourself and that your needs are valid. Replace self-critical thoughts with self-compassionate ones. Embrace the belief that you deserve care, love, and attention, just like anyone else.

5. **Let Go of the Need for Approval**: Recognize that you cannot please everyone, and seeking constant approval can be exhausting and detrimental to your well-being. Accept that it is impossible to meet everyone's expectations and that it is okay to prioritize yourself. Remember that your happiness and well-being are not dependent on others' validation.

6. **Practice Saying No:** Learn to say "no" assertively and without guilt. Understand that saying "no" is not a rejection of others but a way to honour your boundaries and well-being. Trust that those who genuinely care about you will understand and respect your decisions. Practice saying "no" with confidence, knowing that it is an act of self-care and self-respect.

7. **Schedule Self-Care Activities:** Make self-care a non-negotiable part of your routine. Schedule dedicated time for activities that nourish your mind, body, and soul. Engage in activities that bring you joy, relaxation, and rejuvenation. Whether it's practicing mindfulness, taking a bubble bath, pursuing hobbies, or spending time in nature, prioritize these activities without guilt.

8. **Surround Yourself with Supportive Individuals:** Surround yourself with people who understand the importance of self-care and support your journey. Seek out friends, family members, or support groups who uplift and encourage your well-being. Surrounding yourself with like-minded

individuals can help alleviate guilt and reinforce the value of putting yourself first.

Putting yourself first without guilt is a transformative practice that allows you to nurture your well-being and create a balanced, fulfilling life. By understanding the importance of self-care, acknowledging your needs and values, setting boundaries, practicing self-compassion, letting go of the need for approval, saying no with confidence, scheduling self-care activities, and surrounding yourself with supportive individuals, you can embrace the art of prioritizing yourself without guilt. Remember, you deserve to live a life that nourishes and fulfils you, and by prioritizing your own well-being, you can show up as the best version of yourself for others as well.

Exercise : 5

Communicate Openly and Clearly using "I" Statements

Effective communication is essential for building strong and healthy relationships. "I" statements are a powerful tool that can help you express yourself assertively and honestly without sounding accusatory or defensive. By using "I" statements, you take ownership of your feelings and thoughts, making it easier for others to understand your perspective. Here's how to communicate openly and clearly using "I" statements:

1. **Identify Your Emotions:** Before communicating, take a moment to identify and acknowledge your emotions. Be aware of how you feel about the situation or the issue you want to address. This self-awareness will help you articulate your feelings more clearly.

2. **Start with "I Feel":** Begin your statement with "I feel" to express your emotions. For example, instead of saying, "You never listen to me," say, "I feel unheard when I'm trying to share my thoughts."

3. **Be Specific:** Be specific about the behavior or situation that is causing your feelings. This helps the other person understand what triggered your emotions. For example, instead of saying, "You always leave the dishes dirty," say, "I feel overwhelmed when I see dirty dishes in the sink after a long day."

4. **Share the Impact:** Express how the behavior or situation impacts you personally. This allows the other person to empathize with your perspective. For example, instead of saying, "You're so careless," say, "I feel frustrated when things are left disorganized because it makes it hard for me to find what I need."

5. **Avoid Blame and Accusation:** Refrain from blaming or accusing the other person for your feelings. Stay focused on

your emotions and experiences without attacking them. For example, instead of saying, "You're always late, and it's disrespectful," say, "I feel anxious when plans change without notice."

6. **Be Respectful and Calm:** Deliver your "I" statement in a calm and respectful tone. Avoid raising your voice or using offensive language. Approach the conversation with a willingness to listen and understand the other person's perspective as well.

7. **Be Open to Discussion:** After expressing your feelings, invite the other person to share their thoughts and feelings on the matter. Be open to a two-way conversation and be willing to find a resolution together.

Example: Instead of saying, "You never help with household chores," you can say, "I feel overwhelmed when I handle all the household chores alone. It would mean a lot to me if we could share the responsibilities and work together as a team."

Using "I" statements fosters open communication, encourages empathy, and helps prevent misunderstandings. It allows you to assert your feelings while maintaining a respectful and positive dialogue with others. Practice using "I" statements regularly, and you'll find that it improves the quality of your interactions and strengthens your relationships.

CHAPTER 6

BUILDING POSITIVE RELATIONSHIP

Surrounding yourself with supportive and uplifting people is crucial for personal growth, happiness, and overall well-being. The relationships we cultivate and maintain can greatly influence our mindset, motivation, and success. Here are some key points to consider when it comes to surrounding yourself with such individuals:

1. **Positive Influence:** Choose friends and acquaintances who exude positivity and inspire you to become the best version of yourself. Look for people who encourage your dreams, offer constructive feedback, and celebrate your achievements. Positive energy is contagious, and being around those who radiate it can uplift your spirits and help you maintain a positive outlook on life.

2. **Shared Values:** Seek out individuals who share similar values and beliefs. Surrounding yourself with like-minded people creates a sense of belonging and understanding. It fosters an environment where you can openly discuss your thoughts, aspirations, and challenges without fear of judgment. When your values align, you can support and uplift each other as you navigate through life's ups and downs.

3. **Emotional Support:** It's essential to have a support system that provides emotional support during difficult times. Surround yourself with people who genuinely care about your well-being and are willing to lend a listening ear or a comforting shoulder. Having someone who understands your struggles and offers empathy can make a significant difference in your ability to cope with challenges and bounce back stronger.

4. **Encouragement and Motivation:** Look for individuals who genuinely believe in your abilities and offer encouragement and motivation. Whether it's pursuing a new career, starting a business, or learning a new skill, having supportive people around you can boost your confidence and inspire you to push your limits. Their unwavering faith in your potential can serve as a catalyst for personal and professional growth.

5. **Constructive Feedback:** Surrounding yourself with uplifting people doesn't mean surrounding yourself with yes-men or yes-women. It's crucial to have individuals who provide honest and constructive feedback. Constructive criticism helps you identify areas for improvement and refine your skills. Embrace feedback from those who genuinely have your best interests at heart and who can help you grow, even if it might be momentarily uncomfortable.

6. **Celebrating Success:** Choose friends and companions who celebrate your successes and achievements. It's important to have people who cheer you on during your accomplishments, big or small. Their support and recognition can reinforce your self-esteem and motivate you to reach for even greater heights. Likewise, be sure to reciprocate their celebrations and support their endeavours.

Remember, the quality of your relationships plays a significant role in shaping your mindset, aspirations, and overall happiness. Surrounding yourself with supportive and uplifting people creates an environment conducive to personal growth and success.

Be intentional in choosing those who inspire, encourage, and challenge you to become the best version of yourself.

Cultivating authentic connections

Cultivating authentic connections is about creating meaningful and genuine relationships with others. It goes beyond superficial interactions and requires openness, vulnerability, and a willingness to connect on a deeper level. Here are some key aspects to consider when it comes to cultivating authentic connections:

1. **Be Yourself:** Authentic connections thrive when you are true to yourself. Embrace your uniqueness and let your genuine personality shine through. When you are authentic, you attract like-minded individuals who appreciate and accept you for who you truly are. Avoid putting up facades or pretending to be someone you're not, as it can hinder the development of genuine connections.

2. **Active Listening:** Practice active listening when engaging with others. Give your full attention, maintain eye contact, and show genuine interest in what they have to say. This demonstrates that you value their thoughts and feelings. Ask thoughtful questions and encourage them to express themselves further. By actively listening, you create a space for meaningful conversations and establish a deeper connection.

3. **Show Empathy and Understanding:** Cultivate empathy by putting yourself in the other person's shoes and striving to understand their perspective. Be non-judgmental and open-minded, allowing them to express their emotions and experiences without fear of criticism. Genuine connections are built on a foundation of mutual understanding, compassion, and support.

4. **Share Your Vulnerabilities:** Authentic connections require vulnerability. Be willing to share your thoughts, feelings, and experiences with others. By opening up and showing vulnerability, you invite others to do the same. This creates a sense of trust and deepens the connection as both parties feel comfortable being their authentic selves around each other.

5. **Mutual Respect:** Respect is vital in any relationship. Treat others with kindness, compassion, and respect their boundaries. Honor their opinions and choices, even if they differ from your own. Authentic connections thrive when both parties feel valued and respected for who they are.

6. **Invest Time and Effort:** Building authentic connections takes time and effort. It requires nurturing the relationship by spending quality time together, engaging in meaningful conversations, and supporting each other through both joyful and challenging times. Be present and make an effort to maintain regular contact, whether it's through in-person meetings, phone calls, or digital communication.

7. **Seek Common Ground:** Look for shared interests, values, or goals that can form the basis of your connection. Shared experiences and passions create a sense of camaraderie and strengthen the bond between individuals. Engaging in activities or projects together can foster a deeper understanding and connection.

8. **Be Reliable and Trustworthy:** Authentic connections are built on trust and reliability. Be someone others can rely on and trust to keep their confidences. Follow through on your commitments and be there for them when they need support. By being dependable, you establish a solid foundation for a genuine connection.

Cultivating authentic connections is a continual process that requires ongoing effort and sincerity. As you invest in these relationships, you will find that they enrich your life, bring joy, and provide a support system of individuals who truly understand and care about you.

Letting go of toxic relationships and creating space for healthy ones

Letting go of toxic relationships and creating space for healthy ones is essential for your well-being and personal growth. Toxic relationships can drain your energy, hinder your progress, and negatively impact your mental and emotional health. Creating space for healthy relationships involves recognizing toxic dynamics, setting boundaries, and actively seeking out positive connections. Here are some steps to help you let go of toxic relationships and create space for healthier ones:

1. **Identify Toxic Patterns:** Take a step back and objectively assess your relationships. Look for patterns of toxicity such as constant negativity, manipulation, lack of respect, or emotional and verbal abuse. Recognize how these patterns affect your well-being and overall happiness. Acknowledging the toxicity is the first step towards letting go.

2. **Set Boundaries:** Establishing clear boundaries is crucial when dealing with toxic relationships. Determine what behaviour is acceptable to you and communicate your boundaries assertively. Be prepared to enforce those boundaries and distance yourself from individuals who repeatedly violate them. Remember, setting boundaries is an act of self-care and self-respect.

3. **Seek Support:** Reach out to trusted friends, family, or a therapist for support and guidance. Discussing your experiences with someone who understands and cares about your well-being can provide clarity and validation. They can help you gain perspective and offer valuable insights as you navigate the process of letting go.

4. **Practice Self-Care:** Prioritize self-care as you let go of toxic relationships. Engage in activities that nourish your mind, body, and soul. Focus on your well-being by practicing self-compassion, pursuing hobbies you enjoy, engaging in regular exercise, and practicing mindfulness or meditation. Taking care of yourself will boost your resilience and empower you to move forward.

5. **Reflect and Learn:** Take time to reflect on the lessons learned from toxic relationships. Recognize any patterns or red flags that you may have missed in the past. Use this self-reflection to grow and develop a deeper understanding of your own needs and boundaries. This self-awareness will help you make healthier choices in future relationships.

6. **Embrace Positivity:** Surround yourself with positivity and seek out healthy relationships. Engage in activities and communities that align with your values and interests. Participate in groups, clubs, or organizations that foster a supportive and uplifting environment. By actively seeking out positive connections, you create space for healthier relationships to flourish.

7. **Be Open and Authentic:** Approach new relationships with an open mind and heart. Be authentic and true to yourself, allowing others to see the real you. Authenticity attracts genuine connections and ensures that the relationships you build are based on mutual understanding and respect.

8. **Practice Patience:** Creating space for healthy relationships takes time. Be patient with yourself and the process. Understand that it's okay to take breaks and heal from past experiences. Rushing into new relationships may lead to repeating old patterns. Trust that as you let go of toxic relationships and prioritize your well-being, healthy connections will naturally come into your life.

Letting go of toxic relationships and creating space for healthy ones is an act of self-love and growth. It may be challenging at times, but the rewards of cultivating positive and supportive connections are worth it. By surrounding yourself with individuals who uplift and inspire you, you can nurture relationships that contribute positively to your overall happiness and well-being.

10 Self Love Tips

1. Start a morning yoga routine
2. Turn off the TV, pick up a book
3. Keep a Gratitude Journal
4. Listen to inspiring podcasts
5. Take up a creative hobby
6. Make a Vision Board
7. Get Some Fresh Air
8. Meet up with a friend who makes you laugh
9. Have a Clean up & Clear Out
10. Take a long hot bath

Exercise : 6

Every day before going to sleep write at least 5 positive things happens with you in a day or you did some good thing to other in a day:

CHAPTER 7

CELEBRATING YOUR SUCESSES AND PRACTICING GRATITUDE

Acknowledging and celebrating your achievements

Acknowledging and celebrating your achievements is an important practice that boosts self-confidence, reinforces positive behaviour, and enhances your overall well-being. Taking the time to recognize your accomplishments, no matter how big or small, allows you to appreciate your progress and build a foundation for continued success. Here are some steps to effectively acknowledge and celebrate your achievements:

1. **Reflect on Your Journey:** Take a moment to reflect on your journey and how far you have come. Recognize the challenges you have overcome, the efforts you have invested, and the growth you have experienced along the way. By acknowledging your journey, you gain a deeper appreciation for the achievements you have attained.

2. **Set Meaningful Goals:** Establish clear and meaningful goals that align with your values and aspirations. When you set goals that are important to you, achieving them becomes more fulfilling and worthy of celebration. Break your goals

down into smaller milestones, allowing for more frequent moments of acknowledgment and celebration.

3. **Track Your Progress:** Keep track of your progress and accomplishments. Whether through a journal, a checklist, or a visual representation, document your achievements. This tangible record serves as a reminder of how much you have achieved and can motivate you to keep striving for more.

4. **Practice Self-Reflection**: Regularly engage in self-reflection to assess your growth and accomplishments. Ask yourself questions such as: What have I accomplished? How have I improved? What skills have I developed? Acknowledge the positive changes and progress you have made in various aspects of your life.

5. **Celebrate Milestones:** Celebrate both small and significant milestones along your journey. When you reach a goal or complete a milestone, take the time to acknowledge your accomplishment. Treat yourself to something special, indulge in activities that bring you joy, or share the moment with loved ones who support and celebrate your achievements.

6. **Express Gratitude:** Express gratitude for the opportunities, resources, and support that have contributed to your achievements. Gratitude fosters a positive mindset and helps you appreciate the interconnectedness of your accomplishments. Take a moment to thank those who have supported you along the way, recognizing their role in your success.

7. **Share Your Achievements**: Share your achievements with others who will celebrate and appreciate them. Celebrating with loved ones, friends, or mentors not only allows you to bask in the joy of your accomplishments but also inspires and motivates others. Sharing your achievements can create a positive ripple effect and encourage others to pursue their goals.

8. **Self-Celebration Rituals:** Develop personal rituals to celebrate your achievements. It could be writing a letter of self-praise, treating yourself to a favourite activity, or creating a vision board to commemorate your successes. Find rituals that resonate with you and make them a regular practice to honour and celebrate your achievements.

Acknowledging and celebrating your achievements is not about comparison or seeking validation from others. It is about recognizing your progress, embracing your personal growth, and cultivating a positive mindset. By celebrating your achievements, you reinforce your self-worth, boost your confidence, and cultivate a sense of fulfilment on your journey toward continued success.

Finding joy in the life journey

Finding joy in the life journey is about embracing the present moment, appreciating the beauty around you, and cultivating a positive mindset. It involves discovering happiness and fulfilment in both the big milestones and the everyday experiences. Here are some key points to help you find joy in your life journey:

1. **Practice Gratitude:** Cultivate a grateful mindset by acknowledging and appreciating the blessings in your life. Take time each day to reflect on the things you are thankful for, whether it's the love of your family, good health, a beautiful sunset, or the opportunity to pursue your passions. Gratitude shifts your focus toward the positive aspects of life and invites more joy into your journey.

2. **Embrace Mindfulness:** Be fully present in each moment and savour the simple pleasures that surround you. Engage your senses and notice the details—the smell of fresh coffee, the warmth of the sunlight, the sound of laughter. Mindfulness helps you tune in to the richness of life and find joy in the small moments that often go unnoticed.

3. **Pursue Passions:** Discover and pursue activities that bring you joy and ignite your enthusiasm. Whether it's painting, playing an instrument, hiking, or cooking, make time for your passions. Engaging in activities you love infuses your life with purpose and fulfilment, creating moments of joy along your journey.

4. **Seek Meaningful Connections:** Foster meaningful connections with others. Surround yourself with people who inspire, support, and uplift you. Cultivate relationships that bring joy and allow for genuine connections. Engage in deep conversations, share laughter, and create memories together. Meaningful connections with others enhance the joy in your life journey.

5. **Embrace Growth and Learning:** Embrace personal growth and continuous learning as a source of joy. Challenge yourself to step out of your comfort zone, acquire new skills, or explore different perspectives. Each step forward brings a sense of accomplishment and adds excitement and fulfilment to your journey.

6. **Find Beauty in Nature:** Connect with nature and find solace in its beauty. Spend time outdoors, whether it's a walk in the park, a hike in the mountains, or simply sitting by a serene body of water. Nature has a way of grounding us and reminding us of the wonders of the world, sparking joy and awe in our hearts.

7. **Celebrate Milestones and Progress:** Take time to acknowledge and celebrate your achievements, both big and small. Reflect on how far you have come and the progress you have made. Celebrating milestones not only brings joy but also reinforces a positive mindset and motivates you to keep moving forward.

8. **Practice Self-Compassion:** Be kind and gentle with yourself as you navigate your life journey. Embrace self-compassion by acknowledging your strengths, accepting your imperfections,

and treating yourself with love and understanding. Cultivating self-compassion allows you to find joy in self-acceptance and embrace the ups and downs of life with resilience and grace.

Finding joy in the life journey is a mindset and a choice. It's about finding happiness in the present moment, appreciating the journey itself, and nurturing a positive perspective. By cultivating gratitude, embracing mindfulness, pursuing passions, and fostering meaningful connections, you can infuse your life with joy and create a fulfilling and joyful journey.

Cultivating a gratitude practice

Cultivating a gratitude practice is a powerful way to shift your mindset, increase happiness, and enhance your overall well-being. It involves intentionally focusing on the positive aspects of your life and expressing gratitude for them. Here are some steps to help you cultivate a gratitude practice:

1. **Set Aside Dedicated Time:** Allocate specific time each day to reflect on and express gratitude. It can be in the morning, before bed, or any other time that works best for you. Consistency is key in establishing a gratitude practice.

2. **Start with the Basics:** Begin by acknowledging the simple things you might often take for granted. Reflect on the fundamental blessings in your life, such as having a roof over your head, access to clean water, nourishing food, and supportive relationships. Express gratitude for these foundational elements.

3. **Keep a Gratitude Journal:** Maintain a gratitude journal to record your blessings and positive experiences. Each day, write down three to five things you are grateful for. Be specific and detailed in your entries, focusing on the why and how each item or experience brings you joy or appreciation.

4. **Reflect on Challenging Moments:** Embrace the opportunity to find gratitude even in challenging situations. Reflect on difficulties you have faced and consider the lessons learned or personal growth that resulted from them. Express gratitude for the strength, resilience, or newfound perspective gained through those experiences.

5. **Practice Mindful Appreciation:** Engage in mindful appreciation by intentionally noticing the present moment and finding things to be grateful for. Take a few minutes to observe your surroundings, paying attention to the beauty, sounds, or sensations that bring you joy. This practice helps you cultivate gratitude in real-time.

6. **Share Your Gratitude:** Express your gratitude to others. Tell loved ones, friends, or colleagues how much you appreciate them and the positive impact they have had on your life. Genuine expressions of gratitude not only uplift others but also deepen your connection with them.

7. **Gratitude Rituals:** Incorporate gratitude rituals into your daily routine. For example, you can start meals with a moment of gratitude, where you express thanks for the food and the effort that went into preparing it. Establishing rituals helps anchor gratitude as a consistent part of your life.

8. **Shift Focus from "Have to" to "Get to":** Instead of approaching your obligations and responsibilities with a sense of burden, reframe your mindset to one of gratitude. Recognize that you "get to" perform certain tasks or have certain responsibilities, as they provide opportunities for growth, contribute to your well-being, or enable you to make a difference.

9. **Practice Random Acts of Kindness:** Engage in acts of kindness and service toward others. Small gestures, such as offering a compliment, lending a helping hand, or performing acts of charity, can foster gratitude within yourself and generate gratitude from those you help.

10. **Reflect on Gratitude at Day's End:** Before going to bed, take a few moments to reflect on your day and identify specific moments, experiences, or interactions for which you are grateful. Let these thoughts fill your mind as you drift into a peaceful sleep.

Cultivating a gratitude practice is a continuous journey. By intentionally focusing on the positive aspects of your life and expressing gratitude regularly, you can shift your perspective, cultivate a positive mindset, and experience the many benefits that gratitude brings to your well-being.

Exercise : 7

Set serious goals for your Self-Love Journey:

Write good things about you every day:

Write names of your friends or relatives you love the most

Find joy in the small moments that often go unnoticed and make a note

Chase your passion and hobby, list down (for e.g. reading favourite book, your favourite sports, watching movie, swimming, spending time with pets, or go alone for a nature walk):

CHAPTER 8

AFFIRMATIONS AND MANTRAS FOR SELF-LOVE

Remember, affirmations and mantras are most effective when repeated consistently and with genuine belief. Choose the affirmations that resonate with you the most and integrate them into your daily routine. With time and practice, these positive statements will help cultivate a deep sense of self-love and empower you to live a fulfilling and joyful life.

1. I am deserving of love, and I attract loving and positive relationships into my life.
2. I embrace my flaws and imperfections, knowing they make me unique and beautiful.
3. I release the need for validation from others, as I validate and love myself unconditionally.
4. I honour and respect my boundaries, saying no when it serves my well-being and saying yes when it aligns with my values.
5. I am grateful for my journey and trust that everything happens for my highest good.

6. I choose to let go of self-criticism and embrace self-acceptance and self-love.
7. I am proud of myself for how far I have come and excited about the person I am becoming.
8. I forgive myself for any mistakes or perceived failures, knowing that they are opportunities for growth and learning.
9. I prioritize self-care and nourish my mind, body, and soul with love and compassion.
10. I radiate self-confidence and approach challenges with a positive mindset.
11. I am the author of my own story, and I choose to create a life filled with love, joy, and abundance.
12. I release any negative beliefs about myself and replace them with empowering thoughts and beliefs.
13. I am worthy of all the good things that life has to offer, and I open myself up to receiving them.
14. I trust my intuition and make decisions that align with my authentic self.
15. I am enough just as I am, and I embrace my inherent worthiness.
16. I celebrate my achievements, big and small, and acknowledge the effort and dedication I put into reaching my goals.
17. I release comparison and embrace my own unique journey and gifts.
18. I choose to prioritize my happiness and surround myself with people who uplift and inspire me.
19. I am a magnet for positivity and attract positive experiences and opportunities into my life.

20. I love myself unconditionally and treat myself with kindness, compassion, and respect.
21. Here are some more positive affirmations and mantras for self-love:
22. I am worthy of love and acceptance just as I am.
23. I embrace my unique qualities and celebrate my individuality.
24. I choose to love and care for myself unconditionally.
25. I am enough, and I have everything within me to create a life I love.
26. I radiate confidence, positivity, and inner beauty.
27. I am deserving of happiness, abundance, and fulHere are some positive affirmations and mantras for self-love:
28. I am worthy of love and acceptance just as I am.
29. I embrace my unique qualities and celebrate my individuality.
30. I choose to love and care for myself unconditionally.
31. I am enough, and I have everything within me to create a life I love.
32. I radiate confidence, positivity, and inner beauty.
33. I deserve to prioritize my needs and make self-care a priority.
34. I am worthy of success and believe in my unlimited potential.
35. I am worthy of love, both from others and from myself.
36. I am deserving of joy, and I choose to find it in every moment.
37. I let go of comparison and embrace my own unique path.
38. I am grateful for my strengths and embrace areas for growth.
39. I choose thoughts that empower, uplift, and nurture my soul.

40. I am a magnificent being, worthy of all the love and happiness life has to offer.
41. I release all self-judgment and embrace self-compassion.
42. I choose to surround myself with people who uplift and support me.
43. I am grateful for my body and treat it with love and respect.
44. I forgive myself for past mistakes and allow myself to grow and learn.
45. I trust in my abilities and have faith in my journey.
46. I am capable of achieving my dreams and turning them into reality.
47. I deserve to prioritize my needs and make self-care a priority.
48. I am worthy of success and believe in my unlimited potential.
49. I am worthy of love, both from others and from myself.
50. I am deserving of joy, and I choose to find it in every moment.
51. I let go of comparison and embrace my own unique path.
52. I am grateful for my strengths and embrace areas for growth.
53. I choose thoughts that empower, uplift, and nurture my soul.
54. I am a magnificent being, worthy of all the love and happiness life has to offer.
55. I release all self-judgment and embrace self-compassion.
56. I choose to surround myself with people who uplift and support me.
57. I am grateful for my body and treat it with love and respect.
58. I forgive myself for past mistakes and allow myself to grow and learn.

59. I trust in my abilities and have faith in my journey.

60. I release all self-judgment and embrace self-compassion.

61. I choose to surround myself with people who uplift and support me.

62. I am grateful for my body and treat it with love and respect.

63. I forgive myself for past mistakes and allow myself to grow and learn.

64. I trust in my abilities and have faith in my journey.

Feel free to choose the affirmations that resonate with you the most and repeat them daily. By consistently affirming your self-love, you will strengthen your belief in your worthiness and cultivate a deep sense of love and acceptance for yourself.

Mantras to anchor your self-love practice:

Choose the mantras that resonate with you the most and repeat them regularly during your self-love practice. Allow these empowering statements to anchor you in the belief of your worthiness and cultivate a deep sense of love, acceptance, and appreciation for yourself.

Here are some mantras to anchor your self-love practice:

1. I am deserving of love and embrace it fully.
2. I choose to love and accept myself exactly as I am.
3. My self-worth is not dependent on external validation.
4. I am worthy of all the good things life has to offer.
5. I am enough, just as I am, in this very moment.
6. I radiate love, confidence, and inner beauty.

7. I release self-judgment and embrace self-compassion.
8. I am the author of my own happiness, and I choose to love myself unconditionally.
9. My self-love is unwavering, even in the face of challenges.
10. I am a unique and magnificent being, and I embrace my individuality.
11. I am my own best friend, and I treat myself with love and kindness.
12. I trust in my own abilities and have faith in my journey.
13. I am worthy of prioritizing my needs and practicing self-care.
14. I release the need to compare myself to others and embrace my own worthiness.
15. I am worthy of forgiveness and growth, and I embrace them wholeheartedly.
16. I am worthy of receiving love, kindness, and respect from others.
17. I choose to let go of self-limiting beliefs and step into my limitless potential.
18. I am a vessel of love and compassion, and I extend it to myself and others.
19. I am deserving of abundance, joy, and fulfilment in all areas of my life.
20. I release the need to compare myself to others and embrace my own worthiness.
21. I am worthy of forgiveness and growth, and I embrace them wholeheartedly.
22. I am worthy of receiving love, kindness, and respect from others.

23. I choose to let go of self-limiting beliefs and step into my limitless potential.
24. I am a vessel of love and compassion, and I extend it to myself and others.
25. I am deserving of abundance, joy, and fulfilment in all areas of my life.
26. I am grateful for my journey and the lessons it brings, as they contribute to my growth and self-love.

Suggestion: Choose the mantras which resonate with you the most and say them loudly in front of the mirror. It will help to create the aura, and you will feel that energy within yourself.

Using affirmations for self-healing and transformation:

Using affirmations for self-healing and transformation is a powerful practice that can help shift your mindset, release negative patterns, and promote personal growth. Affirmations are positive statements that you repeat to yourself to reinforce new beliefs and invite positive change into your life. Here's how you can effectively use affirmations for self-healing and transformation:

1. **Identify Areas for Healing and Transformation:** Reflect on areas of your life where you desire healing and transformation. It could be emotional healing, releasing limiting beliefs, improving self-confidence, cultivating self-love, or overcoming past traumas. Get clear on the specific areas you want to address through affirmations.

2. **Choose Empowering Affirmations:** Select affirmations that align with your healing and transformation goals. Write down positive statements that counteract negative beliefs or patterns you wish to release. Ensure that your affirmations are in the present tense, positive, and personalized to resonate with your unique journey and aspirations.

3. **Repeat Affirmations Consistently:** Create a routine to repeat your affirmations consistently. Set aside dedicated time each day to recite your affirmations, preferably in a quiet and peaceful environment. You can say them aloud or silently in your mind. Repetition is key to reinforcing new beliefs and rewiring your thought patterns.

4. **Engage Your Senses and Emotions:** As you repeat your affirmations, engage your senses and emotions. Visualize yourself embodying the qualities and experiences described in the affirmations. Feel the emotions associated with them, such as joy, confidence, or healing. Engaging your senses and emotions enhances the effectiveness of the affirmations.

5. **Write and Display Affirmations:** Write your affirmations on sticky notes, index cards, or in a journal. Place them where you can see them daily, such as on your bathroom mirror, computer monitor, or bedside table. Seeing your affirmations regularly reinforces them in your subconscious mind and helps integrate them into your daily life.

6. **Practice Affirmations in Challenging Moments:** Utilize affirmations during challenging moments or when negative thoughts and emotions arise. When you catch yourself engaging in self-doubt or self-criticism, consciously replace those thoughts with empowering affirmations. Redirecting your focus to positive statements helps reframe your mindset and supports healing and transformation.

7. **Believe in the Affirmations:** Trust in the power of your affirmations. Believe that the words you repeat hold transformative energy and have the potential to create positive change in your life. Embrace a mindset of openness and receptivity to allow the affirmations to work their magic.

8. Monitor Progress and Adjust Affirmations: Regularly assess your progress and adjust your affirmations as needed. As you experience healing and transformation, you may find that certain affirmations no longer resonate or that new areas for

growth emerge. Modify your affirmations to align with your evolving needs and aspirations.

The effectiveness of affirmations lies in consistent practice, belief, and the willingness to do the inner work required for healing and transformation. Embrace affirmations as a tool to shift your mindset, release old patterns, and invite positive change into your life. With dedication and patience, affirmations can be a catalyst for profound self-healing and transformation.

EMBRACING SELF-LOVE AS A LIFELONG JOURNEY (SUMMARY)

Patience and Perseverance in Cultivating Self-Love

Cultivating self-love is a journey that requires patience and perseverance. It's essential to approach the process with understanding and a commitment to nurturing yourself. Here are some key points to keep in mind while practicing patience and perseverance in cultivating self-love:

1. **Embrace Self-Compassion:** Be kind and gentle with yourself throughout the journey. Understand that cultivating self-love takes time and effort. Treat yourself with the same compassion you would offer to a dear friend facing similar challenges. Embrace self-compassion as a guiding principle in your practice.
2. **Accept Imperfections:** Recognize that nobody is perfect, and that includes you. Embrace your imperfections and see them as a part of your unique beauty and humanity. Give yourself permission to make mistakes and learn from them, understanding that they are opportunities for growth rather than reflections of your worth.
3. **Set Realistic Expectations:** Have realistic expectations for your progress in cultivating self-love. Understand that self-

love is a lifelong journey, and it's okay to have ups and downs along the way. Don't expect to fully transform your mindset overnight. Celebrate small victories and acknowledge that each step forward, no matter how small, is progress.

4. **Practice Self-Care:** Prioritize self-care as an integral part of cultivating self-love. Engage in activities that nourish your mind, body, and soul. Take time to rest, engage in hobbies you enjoy, practice mindfulness, and care for your physical and emotional well-being. Self-care supports your self-love practice and helps build resilience.

5. **Challenge Negative Self-Talk:** Be aware of your self-talk and challenge negative and self-deprecating thoughts. Replace them with positive and empowering affirmations. Practice self-compassion and treat yourself with love and respect in your thoughts and words. Over time, you'll rewire your inner dialogue to be more supportive and loving.

6. **Seek Support:** Surround yourself with a supportive network of loved ones, friends, or even a therapist who can provide encouragement and guidance on your self-love journey. Sharing your experiences, challenges, and progress with others can offer valuable insights and foster a sense of connection and understanding.

7. **Celebrate Progress:** Acknowledge and celebrate your progress, no matter how small it may seem. Celebrate moments of self-love and self-care, as well as instances when you respond to challenges with greater self-compassion. Recognize and appreciate the steps you take toward nurturing a deeper sense of self-love.

8. **Be Patient with Setbacks:** Setbacks are a natural part of any journey, including the path to self-love. Be patient with yourself during challenging times. Instead of dwelling on setbacks or berating yourself, view them as opportunities for learning and growth. Embrace setbacks as valuable lessons and recommit to your practice with renewed determination.

Cultivating self-love is a lifelong practice that requires patience, perseverance, and self-compassion. Be kind to yourself, celebrate your progress, and be patient with the process. With each step forward, you will deepen your love and acceptance for yourself, leading to greater happiness, resilience, and well-being.

Overcoming Obstacles and Setbacks

Overcoming obstacles and setbacks is an inevitable part of life. It is through facing and navigating these challenges that we grow, learn, and become stronger. Here are some strategies to help you overcome obstacles and setbacks:

1. **Embrace a Growth Mindset:** Adopt a growth mindset that views obstacles as opportunities for growth and learning. Believe in your ability to overcome challenges and see setbacks as temporary roadblocks rather than permanent barriers. Embracing a growth mindset allows you to approach obstacles with resilience and determination.

2. **Reframe Challenges as Opportunities:** Shift your perspective and reframe challenges as opportunities for personal development. Instead of seeing obstacles as burdens, view them as chances to learn, gain new skills, and develop resilience. Seek the lessons within each setback and focus on the potential for growth that lies within them.

3. **Break It Down:** When faced with a daunting obstacle, break it down into smaller, manageable tasks. By focusing on one step at a time, you can maintain momentum and make progress. Celebrate small victories along the way, as they provide motivation and reinforce your ability to overcome challenges.

4. **Seek Support:** Reach out for support when facing obstacles and setbacks. Seek guidance from mentors, friends, or family members who can offer advice, encouragement, and a fresh perspective. Remember, you don't have to face challenges

alone, and the support of others can make a significant difference.

5. **Practice Resilience:** Cultivate resilience by bouncing back from setbacks and staying committed to your goals. Remind yourself of past challenges you have overcome and the strength you demonstrated. Trust in your ability to adapt, learn, and persevere, knowing that setbacks are temporary and part of the journey.

9. **Learn from Setbacks:** Take the time to reflect and learn from setbacks. Identify any patterns or lessons that emerge from the experience. Use setbacks as opportunities to gain insights into your strengths, weaknesses, and areas for improvement. Apply these lessons moving forward to enhance your resilience and decision-making.

10. **Adjust Your Approach:** If a particular approach or strategy is not working, be open to adjusting your course of action. Sometimes, flexibility and adaptability are necessary to overcome obstacles. Consider alternative solutions, seek different perspectives, and be willing to explore new paths to reach your goals.

6. **Practice Self-Care:** Prioritize self-care during challenging times. Take care of your physical, emotional, and mental well-being. Engage in activities that rejuvenate you, such as exercise, spending time in nature, practicing mindfulness, or pursuing hobbies you enjoy. Self-care helps you maintain balance, resilience, and a positive mindset as you navigate obstacles.

7. **Stay Persistent:** Stay persistent and maintain a long-term view of your goals. Understand that setbacks are part of the process, and progress may not always be linear. Stay committed to your vision and keep taking small steps forward, even when faced with challenges. Trust that persistence and perseverance will ultimately lead to success.

Overcoming obstacles and setbacks is a journey that requires patience, resilience, and a positive mindset. By adopting a growth mindset, seeking support, learning from setbacks, and practicing self-care, you can navigate obstacles with resilience and come out stronger on the other side. Embrace challenges as opportunities for growth, and trust in your ability to overcome whatever comes your way.

Sustaining Self-Love and Incorporating It into Your Daily Life

Sustaining self-love and incorporating it into your daily life is an ongoing practice that requires dedication and intention. Here are some strategies to help you cultivate and sustain self-love in your everyday life:

1. **Prioritize Self-Care:** Make self-care a non-negotiable part of your daily routine. Dedicate time to activities that nourish your mind, body, and soul. This can include practicing mindfulness, engaging in physical exercise, getting enough restful sleep, nourishing your body with nutritious food, and indulging in activities that bring you joy and relaxation. Prioritizing self-care sends a powerful message to yourself that you value your well-being.

2. **Practice Self-Compassion:** Be gentle and kind with yourself, especially during challenging times. Treat yourself with the same compassion and understanding you would offer to a dear friend. Acknowledge that you are doing your best, and it's okay to make mistakes and experience setbacks. Self-compassion nourishes your self-love journey and supports your growth and healing.

3. **Set Boundaries:** Establish and communicate clear boundaries in your relationships and daily life. Learn to say no to things that do not align with your values, well-being, or personal priorities. By setting boundaries, you create space for self-care,

self-respect, and self-love. Remember that it is not selfish to prioritize your needs and honor your boundaries.

4. **Challenge Negative Self-Talk:** Notice negative self-talk and actively challenge it. Replace self-criticism with affirmations and positive self-talk. Focus on your strengths, accomplishments, and the qualities that make you unique. Treat yourself with the same kindness and support you would offer to a dear friend. By consciously redirecting negative self-talk, you create space for self-love to flourish.

5. **Surround Yourself with Supportive Relationships:** Cultivate a supportive network of individuals who uplift, inspire, and celebrate your journey of self-love. Surround yourself with people who appreciate and encourage you for who you are. Seek out relationships that foster positivity, acceptance, and personal growth. A strong support system can fuel your self-love practice and provide encouragement during challenging times.

6. **Practice Gratitude:** Incorporate gratitude into your daily life. Take time each day to reflect on the things you are grateful for, both big and small. Acknowledge and appreciate the blessings, experiences, and qualities that bring joy to your life. Gratitude fosters a positive mindset and shifts your focus towards the abundance and love that surrounds you, reinforcing your self-love practice.

7. **Engage in Self-Reflection:** Regularly engage in self-reflection to gain deeper insights into your thoughts, emotions, and patterns of behaviour. Set aside time to journal, meditate, or engage in introspective practices that help you understand yourself better. Self-reflection enhances self-awareness, which is crucial for sustained self-love and personal growth.

8. **Celebrate Your Achievements:** Acknowledge and celebrate your achievements, big and small. Take time to recognize your progress and the steps you have taken towards self-love.

Celebrate moments of self-compassion, self-acceptance, and self-growth. By celebrating your achievements, you reinforce the belief in your worthiness and strengthen your self-love practice.

Remember, sustaining self-love is a daily practice that requires consistent effort and self-awareness. By prioritizing self-care, practicing self-compassion, setting boundaries, surrounding yourself with support, and engaging in gratitude and self-reflection, you can weave self-love into the fabric of your daily life. Embrace self-love as an ongoing journey and commitment to your well-being and happiness.

Embrace Yourself: A Lifetime of Self-Love

Self-love is a lifelong journey, an ongoing commitment to accepting, embracing, and nurturing your authentic self. It's about cultivating a deep sense of love, compassion, and appreciation for who you are at your core. Here are some key points to remember as you embark on this beautiful journey of self-love:

1. **Embrace Imperfections:** Recognize that imperfections are what make you unique and beautiful. Embrace your quirks, flaws, and vulnerabilities as part of your individuality. Love yourself fully, including the parts you might have once considered shortcomings. Embracing your imperfections allows you to fully accept and appreciate yourself.

2. **Practice Self-Compassion:** Be gentle and kind with yourself, especially during challenging times. Treat yourself with the same compassion and understanding you would offer to a dear friend. Acknowledge that you are doing your best, and it's okay to make mistakes and experience setbacks. Self-compassion nourishes your self-love journey and supports your growth and healing.

3. **Cultivate Positive Self-Talk:** Be mindful of your self-talk and choose words that uplift and empower you. Replace self-

criticism with self-affirmation. Speak to yourself with kindness, love, and encouragement. Positive self-talk nourishes self-love and helps reframe your mindset to focus on your strengths and inner beauty.

4. **Set Boundaries:** Establish clear boundaries to protect your well-being and maintain healthy relationships. Learn to say no to things that deplete your energy or compromise your values. Surround yourself with people who respect and support your boundaries. Setting boundaries reinforces self-love and ensures that you create a space where your needs are honored.

5. **Embrace Growth and Self-Reflection:** Embrace personal growth as an integral part of your self-love journey. Engage in self-reflection, explore your emotions, and challenge limiting beliefs. Be open to learning, evolving, and expanding your horizons. Embracing growth allows you to continually deepen your self-love and step into your highest potential.

6. **Practice Gratitude:** Cultivate gratitude for yourself and your life. Take time to appreciate the qualities, experiences, and opportunities that have shaped you into who you are. Express gratitude for the lessons learned from challenges and the growth that has occurred. Gratitude fuels self-love and shifts your focus towards abundance and positivity.

7. **Celebrate Your Uniqueness:** Embrace your unique gifts, talents, and passions. Celebrate what makes you different from others. Honor your journey and the progress you've made. Recognize that your uniqueness is something to be cherished and celebrated. Embracing your individuality strengthens your self-love and allows you to shine your light brightly in the world.

Remember, self-love is not a destination but a lifelong practice. Embrace yourself with love, compassion, and acceptance every step of the way. Embrace the journey of self-discovery, growth, and transformation. Embrace yourself fully, for you are deserving of a lifetime filled with self-love, joy, and fulfillment.

HERE ARE SOME ADDITIONAL RESOURCES AND REFERENCES THAT CAN SUPPORT YOUR JOURNEY OF SELF-LOVE

Books:

8. "The Gifts of Imperfection" by Brené Brown
9. "Radical Self-Love: A Guide to Loving Yourself and Living Your Dreams" by Gala Darling
10. "Love Yourself Like Your Life Depends On It" by Kamal Ravikant
11. "The Self-Love Experiment: Fifteen Principles for Becoming More Kind, Compassionate, and Accepting of Yourself" by Shannon Kaiser
12. "The Body Is Not an Apology: The Power of Radical Self-Love" by Sonya Renee Taylor
13. "The Mastery of Love: A Practical Guide to the Art of Relationship" by Don Miguel Ruiz
14. "You Can Heal Your Life" by Louise Hay

15. "The Power of Now: A Guide to Spiritual Enlightenment" by Eckhart Tolle
16. Websites and Online Resources:
17. Tiny Buddha (www.tinybuddha.com): Offers articles, stories, and resources on self-love, mindfulness, and personal growth.
18. Self-Compassion (self-compassion.org): Provides information, exercises, and guided meditations on self-compassion, developed by Dr. Kristin Neff.
19. Mindful (www.mindful.org): Features articles and resources on mindfulness, self-care, and emotional well-being.
20. Psychology Today (www.psychologytoday.com): Offers a wide range of articles and resources on self-love, self-esteem, and mental health.
21. The Self-Love Workbook (www.theselflove.com): A website dedicated to self-love and personal growth, featuring articles, exercises, and tools for self-reflection.

Podcasts:

22. "The Love, Happiness and Success Podcast" by Dr. Lisa Marie Bobby
23. "The Life Coach School Podcast" by Brooke Castillo
24. "The Self-Love Fix" by Beatrice Kamau
25. "The School of Greatness" by Lewis Howes
26. "The Mindful Kind" by Rachael Kable

These resources can provide further insights, inspiration, and practical guidance on your self-love journey. Remember to explore what resonates with you and adapt the concepts and practices to suit your unique needs and preferences. Your journey of self-love is personal, and these resources can serve as valuable tools to support and empower you along the way.

The self-love journey is a deeply personal and transformative process of cultivating love, acceptance, and compassion for oneself. It involves embracing imperfections, practicing self-care, setting boundaries, and nurturing a positive mindset. Throughout the journey, individuals learn to let go of self-criticism, comparison, and seeking validation from others. Instead, they prioritize their well-being, honour their needs, and celebrate their unique qualities and accomplishments. The self-love journey is not a destination but a lifelong practice of growth, self-reflection, and embracing authenticity. It empowers individuals to live authentically, radiate confidence, and create a life filled with love, joy, and fulfilment.

The journey of self-love is a transformative process that holds immense importance in enhancing overall happiness, well-being, and personal growth. Through self-acceptance, self-compassion, self-care, setting healthy boundaries, cultivating positive self-talk, and embracing authenticity, we nurture a profound connection with ourselves.

By valuing and loving ourselves unconditionally, we create a solid foundation for a joyful, meaningful, and fulfilling life. Embrace the journey of self-love and experience the transformative power it can bring to every aspect of your being.

Make your self-love journey more powerful and impactful by using these practical daily rituals:

Morning Daily Rituals for Practicing Self-Love

Starting your day with intentional self-love rituals can set a positive tone for the rest of your day. Here are some morning rituals you can incorporate into your daily routine to nurture self-love:

1. **Gratitude Practice:** Begin your day by expressing gratitude for the blessings in your life. Take a few moments to reflect on the things you are thankful for, whether it's your loved ones, your health, the opportunities you have, or simply the gift of a new day. Write them down in a gratitude journal or silently express them in your mind.

2. **Mindful Breathing or Meditation:** Set aside a few minutes for mindful breathing or meditation. Find a quiet space where you can sit comfortably, close your eyes, and focus on your breath. Pay attention to each inhale and exhale, allowing yourself to be fully present in the moment. If meditation feels challenging, you can use guided meditation apps or listen to calming music to assist you.

3. **Positive Affirmations:** Repeat positive affirmations that resonate with you. Choose affirmations that reflect self-love, self-acceptance, and confidence. Speak them aloud or silently to yourself, reinforcing empowering beliefs about yourself and your abilities. Some examples include "I am worthy of love and happiness," "I am enough just as I am," or "I embrace my true authentic self with love and compassion."

4. **Gentle Stretching or Yoga:** Engage in gentle stretching or a short yoga practice to awaken your body and mind. Focus on gentle movements that help release tension and promote flexibility. Pay attention to how your body feels and honor its needs. This practice allows you to connect with your physical self and cultivate a loving relationship with your body.

5. **Nourishing Breakfast:** Prepare and enjoy a nourishing breakfast. Choose foods that fuel your body and make you feel good. Take the time to savor each bite, being mindful of the nourishment you're providing yourself. Eating with intention and appreciation fosters a positive relationship with food and nourishes your body from the inside out.

6. **Affectionate Self-Care:** Engage in a self-care ritual that feels loving and nurturing to you. This could involve taking a relaxing bath, pampering your skin, practicing gentle self-massage, or engaging in a self-care activity that brings you joy. The key is to prioritize your well-being and show yourself the same care and attention you would give to someone you love.

7. **Setting Intentions:** Take a few moments to set positive intentions for the day ahead. Reflect on how you want to show up, the energy you want to bring into your interactions, and the mindset you want to cultivate. Set intentions that align with self-love, such as choosing kindness, embracing self-compassion, or seeking opportunities for personal growth.

Remember, these rituals are meant to be personalized to your preferences and needs. Experiment with different practices and find what resonates with you. The key is to approach these rituals with presence, intention, and a genuine desire to nurture and cultivate self-love.

By starting your day with self-love rituals, you create a foundation for a positive and fulfilling journey of self-care and personal growth.

Bedtime Rituals for Practicing Self-Love

Establishing a bedtime routine that prioritizes self-love and self-care can promote a sense of calm, relaxation, and inner peace. Here are some bedtime rituals you can incorporate into your routine to nurture self-love:

1. **Digital Detox:** Disconnect from electronic devices at least 30 minutes before bedtime. Put away your phone, tablet, or laptop and create a screen-free environment. This allows you to wind down and create a space for relaxation and self-reflection.

2. **Gentle Stretching or Yoga:** Engage in gentle stretching or a short yoga practice before bed. This can help release tension from the day and promote relaxation. Focus on gentle movements, deep breathing, and stretching areas of tightness in your body. Tune in to the sensations and let go of any lingering stress or physical discomfort.

3. **Journaling:** bed. This can be a space to express your thoughts, emotions, or reflections on the day. Write about the things you're grateful for, the lessons learned, or anything that comes to mind. Journaling provides a therapeutic outlet and helps you process your experiences, fostering self-awareness and self-reflection.

4. **Mindfulness or Meditation:** Practice mindfulness or meditation as part of your bedtime routine. Find a quiet and comfortable space where you can sit or lie down. Focus on your breath or use guided meditation apps to help quiet your mind and relax your body. Allow yourself to fully be present in the moment and let go of any worries or stress.

5. **Self-Care Rituals:** Engage in soothing self-care rituals that promote relaxation and self-nurturing. This could involve taking a warm bath with essential oils, practicing a skincare routine with gentle products, or using calming aromatherapy to create a peaceful atmosphere. Choose activities that make you feel cared for and nurtured.

6. **Gratitude Reflection:** Before drifting off to sleep, reflect on the things you are grateful for. Consider the positive moments, experiences, or interactions from the day. Express gratitude for the lessons learned and the progress made. Cultivating a mindset of gratitude helps shift your focus towards positivity and fosters a sense of contentment.

7. **Affirmations or Self-Love Mantras:** Repeat affirmations or self-love mantras as you settle into bed. Choose statements that reinforce self-love, self-acceptance, and inner peace. Speak them softly to yourself, allowing the words to sink in

and resonate. Affirmations help reprogram your subconscious mind and cultivate a positive self-image.

8. **Restful Sleep Environment:** Create a sleep-friendly environment that promotes restful sleep. Ensure your bedroom is dark, quiet, and at a comfortable temperature. Use soft, comfortable bedding and pillows that support your body. Prioritize quality sleep as an act of self-love, allowing your body and mind to rejuvenate and replenish.

Remember, the key to bedtime rituals is to create a routine that supports your well-being and helps you transition into a restful state. Customize these rituals to suit your preferences and needs. By incorporating self-love practices into your bedtime routine, you can cultivate a deeper sense of self-care, inner peace, and overall well-being.

Self-Love Journal: Daily Practice

Keeping a self-love journal can be a powerful tool for cultivating self-awareness, practicing self-compassion, and nurturing your relationship with yourself. It provides a safe space to explore your thoughts, emotions, and experiences, and to celebrate your journey of self-love. Here's a framework for a self-love journaling practice:

1. **Start with Gratitude:** Begin each entry by expressing gratitude for the day or for specific blessings in your life. Write down three things you are grateful for, focusing on moments, people, or experiences that bring you joy and appreciation. Gratitude sets a positive tone and shifts your mindset towards positivity and abundance.

2. **Reflect on Your Feelings:** Take a moment to tune into your emotions and reflect on how you're feeling. Write freely about any thoughts or emotions that arise. This reflection allows you to acknowledge and validate your feelings, fostering self-awareness and emotional well-being.

3. **Celebrate Victories:** Celebrate your achievements and victories, no matter how big or small. Write about the progress you've made, the obstacles you've overcome, or the moments when you practiced self-love. Celebrating your victories reinforces self-appreciation and reminds you of your capacity for growth and resilience.

4. **Release Self-Criticism:** Identify any self-critical thoughts or limiting beliefs that arise. Challenge them by writing counterarguments or reframing them with self-compassionate and empowering statements. Replace self-criticism with self-love and acceptance, offering yourself kind and supportive words.

5. **Practice Affirmations:** Write down positive affirmations that reflect self-love and self-acceptance. Choose statements that resonate with you and feel empowering. Write them as "I am" statements to affirm your worth and potential. For example, "I am worthy of love and respect" or "I embrace my uniqueness and shine my light."

6. **Set Intentions:** Set intentions for the day or reflect on how you want to show up for yourself. Write down intentions that align with self-love and self-care, such as prioritizing self-care activities, setting healthy boundaries, or practicing self-compassion. Intentions provide guidance and focus for your self-love journey.

7. **Daily Self-Care Practice:** Document your self-care activities for the day. Write about the self-nurturing actions you took, whether it's engaging in a hobby, practicing mindfulness, going for a walk, or expressing creativity. Acknowledge the efforts you made to prioritize self-care and self-love.

8. **Reflection and Release:** Reflect on the day's experiences and any lessons learned. Write about any insights or moments of growth that emerged. If there are any challenges or negative experiences, consider what you can learn from them and how you can offer yourself kindness and support moving forward.

Release any lingering negative emotions by writing them down and allowing yourself to let go.

9. **End with Self-Compassion:** Conclude each journal entry with words of self-compassion and love. Offer yourself gentle reminders of your worthiness, resilience, and capacity for growth. Write a loving message to yourself, encouraging and nurturing your inner self.

Remember, there are no rules or restrictions when it comes to journaling. Customize this practice to suit your needs and preferences. Make it a daily habit to connect with yourself and cultivate self-love. Your self-love journal is a personal space for self-exploration, healing, and growth. Embrace this practice as a powerful tool in your journey of self-love and self-discovery.

Wishing Statement for Self-Love Journey

May my future self embark on a profound and transformative journey of self-love, embracing every step of the way with compassion, courage, and grace. May I cultivate a deep sense of love and acceptance for myself, recognizing my worthiness and inherent beauty as I am.

I wish for my future self to release any self-doubt and limiting beliefs, replacing them with empowering thoughts that celebrate my uniqueness and strengths. May I let go of past hurts and resentments, allowing forgiveness to heal my heart and pave the way for a brighter, more loving future.

May I prioritize self-care and self-nurturing, understanding that I am deserving of kindness and tenderness. Let me embrace the importance of setting healthy boundaries, honouring my needs, and valuing my time and energy.

In the journey of self-love, I wish for my future self to cultivate a positive mindset, anchoring myself in gratitude and abundance.

May I embrace each day with a grateful heart, celebrating the joys and growth that come with each experience.

I wish for my future self to embrace authenticity and fearlessly show up as my true self. Let me shine my light brightly, unapologetically, and attract meaningful connections and experiences that align with my soul's purpose.

May my future self navigate challenges with resilience and self-compassion, recognizing that every setback is an opportunity for growth. I wish to embrace change with open arms, knowing that each chapter of my journey contributes to my evolution and self-discovery.

I wish for my future self to celebrate my achievements, big and small, acknowledging my progress and honouring the efforts I invest in my self-love journey. May I be my own greatest cheerleader, reminding myself of the boundless potential that resides within me.

Above all, I wish for my future self to nurture an unwavering love for myself, holding space for my emotions, dreams, and aspirations. May I treat myself with the same gentleness and love I extend to others, knowing that I am deserving of the infinite love that exists within me.

With an open heart and a determined spirit, I set forth on this self-love journey, embracing the limitless possibilities that await me. May I experience the profound joy and freedom that comes from loving myself unconditionally.

I trust that my future self will continue to blossom in love, radiating light and positivity to those around me. And so, I release this wish into the universe, knowing that the seeds of self-love have been sown, and the journey ahead will be one of growth, healing, and boundless love.